Prozac and Other Antidepressants

JUNIOR DRUG AWARENESS

JUNIOR DRUG AWARENESS

Prozac and Other Antidepressants

Tara Koellhoffer

CHELSEA HOUSE
PUBLISHERS
An imprint of Infobase Publishing

Chelsea House
An imprint of Infobase Publishing
132 West 31st Street
New York NY 10001

Library of Congress Cataloging-in-Publication Data

Koellhoffer, Tara.
   Prozac and other antidepressants / Tara Koellhoffer.
      p. cm. — (Junior drug awareness)
   Includes bibliographical references and index.
   ISBN 978-0-7910-9747-2 (hardcover)
      1. Antidepressants—Juvenile literature.   2. Fluoxetine—Juvenile literature.
   I. Title.   II. Series.

   RM332.K64 2008
   615'.78—dc22   2007043663

Chelsea House books are available at special discounts when purchased in bulk quantities for businesses, associations, institutions, or sales promotions. Please call our Special Sales Department in New York at (212) 967-8800 or (800) 322-8755.

You can find Chelsea House on the World Wide Web at http://www.chelseahouse.com

Text design by Erik Lindstrom
Cover design by Jooyoung An

Printed in the United States

Bang NMSG 10 9 8 7 6 5 4 3 2 1

This book is printed on acid-free paper.

All links and web addresses were checked and verified to be correct at the time of publication. Because of the dynamic nature of the web, some addresses and links may have changed since publication and may no longer be valid.

CONTENTS

Battling a Pandemic: A History of Drugs in the United States

When Johnny came marching home again after the Civil War, he probably wasn't marching in a very straight line. This is because Johnny, like 400,000 of his fellow drug-addled soldiers, was addicted to morphine. With the advent of morphine and the invention of the hypodermic needle, drug addiction became a prominent problem during the nineteenth century. It was the first time such widespread drug dependence was documented in history.

Things didn't get much better in the later decades of the nineteenth century. Cocaine and opiates were used as over-the-counter "medicines." Of course, the most famous was Coca-Cola, which actually did contain cocaine in its early days.

After the turn of the twentieth century, drug abuse was spiraling out of control, and the United States government stepped in with the first regulatory controls. In 1906, the Pure Food and Drug Act became a law. It required the labeling of product ingredients. Next came the Harrison Narcotics Tax Act of 1914, which outlawed illegal importation or distribution of cocaine and opiates. During this time, neither the medical community nor the general population was aware of the principles of addiction.

After the passage of the Harrison Act, drug addiction was not a major issue in the United States until the 1960s, when drug abuse became a much bigger social problem. During this time, the federal government's drug enforcement agencies were found to be ineffective. Organizations often worked against one another, causing counterproductive effects. By 1973, things had gotten so bad that President Richard Nixon, by executive order, created the Drug Enforcement Administration (DEA), which became the lead agency in all federal narcotics investigations. It continues in that role to this day. The effectiveness of enforcement and the so-called "Drug War" are open to debate. Cocaine use has been reduced by 75% since its peak in 1985. However, its replacement might be methamphetamine (speed, crank, crystal), which is arguably more dangerous and is now plaguing the country. Also, illicit drugs tend to be cyclical, with various drugs, such as LSD, appearing, disappearing, and then reappearing again. It is probably closest to the truth to say that a war on drugs can never be won, just managed.

Fighting drugs involves a three-pronged battle. Enforcement is one prong. Education and prevention is the second. Treatment is the third.

Although pandemics of drug abuse have been with us for more than 150 years, education and prevention were not seriously considered until the 1970s. In 1982, former First Lady Betty Ford made drug treatment socially acceptable with the opening of the Betty Ford Center. This followed her own battle with addiction. Other treatment centers—including Hazelden, Fair Oaks, and Smithers (now called the Addiction Institute of New York)—added to the growing number of clinics, and soon detox facilities were in almost every city. The cost of a single day in one of these facilities is often more than $1,000, and the effectiveness of treatment centers is often debated. To this day, there is little regulation over who can practice counseling.

It soon became apparent that the most effective way to deal with the drug problem was prevention by education. By some estimates, the overall cost of drug abuse to society exceeds $250 billion per year; preventive education is certainly the most cost-effective way to deal with the problem. Drug education can save people from misery, pain, and ultimately even jail time or death. In the early 1980s, First Lady Nancy Reagan started the "Just Say No" program. Although many scoffed at the program, its promotion of total abstinence from drugs has been effective with many adolescents. In the late 1980s, drug education was not science-based, and people essentially were throwing mud at the wall to see what would stick. Motivations of all types spawned hundreds, if not thousands, of drug-education programs. Promoters of some programs used whatever political clout they could muster to get on various government agencies' lists of most effective programs. The bottom line, however, is that prevention is very difficult to quantify. It's nearly impossible to prove that drug use would have occurred if it were not prevented from happening.

In 1983, the Los Angeles Unified School District, in conjunction with the Los Angeles Police Department, started what was considered at that time to be the gold standard of school-based drug education programs. The program was called Drug Abuse Resistance Education, otherwise known as D.A.R.E. The program called for specially trained police officers to deliver drug-education programs in schools. This was an era in which community-oriented policing was all the rage. The logic was that kids would give street credibility to a police officer who spoke to them about drugs. The popularity of the program was unprecedented. It spread all across the country and around the world. Ultimately, 80% of American school districts would utilize the program. Parents, police officers, and kids all loved it. Unexpectedly, a special bond was formed between the kids who took the program and the police officers who ran it. Even in adulthood, many kids remember the name of their D.A.R.E. officer.

By 1991, national drug use had been halved. In any other medical-oriented field, this figure would be astonishing. The number of people in the United States using drugs went from about 25 million in the early 1980s to 11 million in 1991. All three prongs of the battle against drugs vied for government dollars, with each prong claiming credit for the reduction in drug use. There is no doubt that each contributed to the decline in drug use, but most people agreed that preventing drug abuse before it started had proved to be the most effective strategy. The National Institute on Drug Abuse (NIDA), which was established in 1974, defines its mandate in this way: "NIDA's mission is to lead the Nation in bringing the power of science to bear on drug abuse and addiction." NIDA leaders were the experts in prevention and treatment, and they had enormous resources. In

1986, the nonprofit Partnership for a Drug-Free America was founded. The organization defined its mission as, "Putting to use all major media outlets, including TV, radio, print advertisements and the Internet, along with the pro bono work of the country's best advertising agencies." The Partnership for a Drug-Free America is responsible for the popular campaign that compared "your brain on drugs" to fried eggs.

The American drug problem was front-page news for years up until 1990–1991. Then the Gulf War took over the news, and drugs never again regained the headlines. Most likely, this lack of media coverage has led to some peaks and valleys in the number of people using drugs, but there has not been a return to anything near the high percentage of use recorded in 1985. According to the University of Michigan's 2006 "Monitoring the Future" study, which measured adolescent drug use, there were 840,000 fewer American kids using drugs in 2006 than in 2001. This represents a 23% reduction in drug use. With the exception of prescription drugs, drug use continues to decline.

In 2000, the Robert Wood Johnson Foundation recognized that the D.A.R.E. Program, with its tens of thousands of trained police officers, had the top state-of-the-art delivery system of drug education in the world. The foundation dedicated $15 million to develop a cutting-edge prevention curriculum to be delivered by D.A.R.E. The new D.A.R.E. program incorporates the latest in prevention and education, including high-tech, interactive, and decision-model-based approaches. D.A.R.E. officers are trained as "coaches" who support kids as they practice research-based refusal strategies in high-stakes peer-pressure environments. Through stunning magnetic resonance imaging (MRI) images, students get to see tangible proof of how various substances diminish brain activity.

Will this program be the solution to the drug problem in the United States? By itself, probably not. It is simply an integral part of a larger equation that everyone involved hopes will prevent kids from ever starting to use drugs. The equation also requires guidance in the home, without which no program can be effective.

Ronald J. Brogan
Regional Director
D.A.R.E America

1

What Is Depression?

For years, Gillian didn't realize that she was depressed. She had a degree in psychology. She knew what the symptoms of depression were. Still, she just thought she was feeling down. As she put it when she posted her story online, "Everyone gets low moods, so I assumed that was all I was feeling." Sometimes Gilllian felt so sad that she could barely drag herself out of bed. But she didn't think she was depressed. Then a friend told Gillian about her own low moods. Gillian realized that the way she was feeling wasn't normal. She saw her doctor and was diagnosed with clinical depression. Gillian started to take Prozac, a well-known **antidepressant** drug. Soon, she felt much better. Eventually, Gillian was able to stop taking Prozac. Her depression has not returned. She says, "I won't let it [depression] steal my life again."

WHAT IS DEPRESSION?

Everybody feels "depressed" now and then. Feeling down is a normal response to the bad things that happen in life, such as the loss of a loved one or a failure at work or school. This "depressed" feeling, however, is not the same as clinical depression.

Clinical depression is a medical illness with multiple causes. The causes are biological, environmental, psychological, and genetic. Clinical depression is also called major depression, major depressive illness, major affective disorder, or **unipolar** mood disorder. Depression causes changes in mood, behavior, energy, and thoughts. It affects the entire body, but it occurs mostly in the brain. People with depression have an imbalance of chemicals in the brain called **neurotransmitters**. Neurotransmitters are chemical messengers that allow the brain cells, or **neurons**, to talk to each other. When someone's neurotransmitters are out of balance, he or she may experience the physical and psychological symptoms of depression. These include changes in sleep patterns and energy level, slowed thinking, changes in appetite, irritability, guilt, and feelings of hopelessness.

Scientists believe that these chemical imbalances in the brain are the primary cause of depression. There is also some evidence that some depressed people have brains that are shaped differently. One study found that young people with depression have less tissue in the **prefrontal cortex** (part of the front of the brain) than nondepressed people do. Other studies have found that parts of the prefrontal cortex are more active in depressed people. These parts are related to emotions and obsessive thoughts. This may explain why depressed people have mood changes and thoughts of sadness and death.

Depression is quite common. Still, many people don't realize they need treatment. Depression can come on little by little. Gradually, it can make a person feel as if life has no meaning or is not worth living.

DEPRESSION THROUGHOUT HISTORY

Depression has existed as long as humans have. Historians have found evidence of depression in ancient times. For the past three thousand years, the descriptions of depression found in various cultures have been remarkably consistent.

A famous document from ancient Egypt, known as the Ebers Papyrus, mentions a condition in which the sufferer feels **despondent**. In ancient Greece, the poet Homer (who wrote *The Iliad* and *The Odyssey*) wrote about a character named Ajax, who became so depressed that he committed suicide. In the Old Testament of the Bible, King Saul is described as severely depressed. Saul also killed himself.

In the fifth century B.C., depression was called **melancholia**. The Greek physician Hippocrates described it as "a persistent sadness and morbid thoughts that had their source in a disorder of the brain." First-century physician Arateus also described depression. He wrote, "In certain of these cases there is mere anger and grief and sad dejection of mind. . . ." First-century Greek writer Plutarch described the way a person with depression felt and behaved:

Every little evil is magnified by the scaring **specters** of his anxiety. He looks on himself as a man whom the gods hate and pursue with their anger. . . . Awake, he makes no use of reason; and asleep, he enjoys no respite from his alarms. His reason always slumbers; his fears are always awake. Nowhere can he find escape from his imaginary terrors.

From the tenth to the eighteenth century, Europeans believed that all mental problems—including depression—were caused by demons or witchcraft. But even centuries ago, some physicians believed that depression was a disease. In 1586, British physician Timothy Bright wrote that depression was a "natural" mental disorder that occurred because of "the mind's apprehension." Not until the twentieth century, however, did most medical researchers begin to accept the idea that depression and other psychological disorders had biological causes and could be treated with medications.

TYPES OF DEPRESSION

In addition to major depression, there are several other forms of depressive illness. Major depression is characterized by at least one depressive episode. A depressive episode means a person has five or more of the symptoms of depression, and that these symptoms last for at least two weeks. The symptoms include:

- Changes in sleep patterns
- Changes in appetite
- Long-lasting sadness or unexplained crying
- Anger, worry, irritability, anxiety, or agitation
- Not caring about anything
- Feeling gloomy; often being negative about things
- Feeling worthless or guilty
- Feeling tired or having low energy
- Problems making decisions

(continues on page 18)

FAMOUS PEOPLE NOTED TO HAVE DEPRESSION

Many famous people have depression or related illnesses, such as bipolar disorder. In fact, some scientists believe that there is a link between depressive illness (especially bipolar disorder) and creativity.

Among the famous people who have reportedly or admittedly suffered from some form of depressive illness are:

- **Abraham Lincoln** (sixteenth president of the United States)
- **Adam Ant** (musician)
  —*"I have suffered from depression for most of my life. It is an illness."*
- **Billy Joel** (musician)
- **Brooke Shields** (actress)
  —*"I was able to get help and I was able to have a support system and recognize [the postpartum depression] relatively early."*
- **Buzz Aldrin** (astronaut)
- **Charles Dickens** (writer)
- **Diana, Princess of Wales**
  —*"You'd wake up in the morning feeling you didn't want to get out of bed, you felt misunderstood, and just very, very low in yourself."*
- **Ernest Hemingway** (writer)
- **Harrison Ford** (actor)
- **Isaac Newton** (scientist)
- **Jim Carrey** (comedian, actor)
- **John Keats** (poet)
  —*"I am in that temper that if I were under water I would scarcely kick to come to the top."*

Nine-time Grammy Award–winning rocker Sheryl Crow has battled depression since childhood. The singer-songwriter is just one of many famous people with depression. She has said in interviews that she uses a combination of antidepressants and therapy to help combat the disease.

- **Leo Tolstoy** (writer)
- **Ludwig von Beethoven** (composer)
- **Michelangelo** (artist)
- **Mike Wallace** (newscaster)
  —*"The sunshine means nothing to you at all. The seasons, friends, good food mean nothing. All you focus on is yourself and how bad you feel."*
- **Patty Duke** (actress)
- **Sheryl Crow** (musician)
  —*"I grew up in the presence of melancholy, a feeling of loss over things that maybe I don't have or never had. . . . It is a shadow for me. It's part of who I am. It is constantly there. I just know how, at this point, to sort of manage it."*

(continues on page 18)

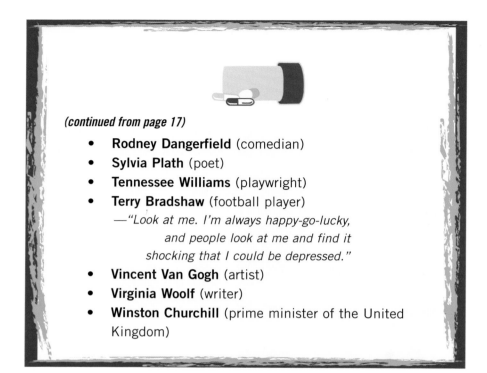

(continued from page 17)
- **Rodney Dangerfield** (comedian)
- **Sylvia Plath** (poet)
- **Tennessee Williams** (playwright)
- **Terry Bradshaw** (football player)
  —*"Look at me. I'm always happy-go-lucky, and people look at me and find it shocking that I could be depressed."*
- **Vincent Van Gogh** (artist)
- **Virginia Woolf** (writer)
- **Winston Churchill** (prime minister of the United Kingdom)

(continued from page 15)
- Problems concentrating
- Avoiding other people
- Not enjoying things you used to like
- Unexplained pain
- Thoughts of death or suicide

These symptoms also mark several other depression-related disorders, including dysthymia, bipolar disorder, seasonal affective disorder, and postpartum depression.

Dysthymia

People with **dysthymia** have some symptoms of depression, but the symptoms are less severe and may last longer.

Approximately 3% to 6% of people have dysthymia. This condition is diagnosed when a person has had symptoms of depression for more than two years and has not been without symptoms for longer than two months of that time. The symptoms of major depression and dysthymia do overlap. However, people with dysthymia don't suffer from weight changes or sleep disturbances as often as those with major depression do. Most dysthymia symptoms are psychological, not physical. Many people with dysthymia don't realize they have it. They often think that the symptoms, such as lack of energy and pessimism, are just a part of their personality.

Bipolar Disorder

Bipolar disorder is not as common as major depression. Bipolar disorder is sometimes called manic-depressive illness or manic-depression. It affects about 1.2% of

PHYSICAL SYMPTOMS OF DEPRESSION

Depression is primarily known as an illness of the brain. Many people don't realize that depressed people often have physical symptoms—and sometimes suffer pain. In 2004, researchers found that two of every three people with depression felt physical pain. The types of pain included joint aches, back and abdominal pain, and repeated headaches. Some people still felt the pain after they went on antidepressants. The researchers said that doctors might be able to use these physical symptoms to help them decide how well depression treatment is working. Even if a person no longer feels depressed, he or she may still have physical symptoms. This could mean that treatment is not working as well as it could be.

Twenty-four-year-old Iraq War veteran Jesus Bocanegra takes four anti-depression and anxiety drugs for post-traumatic stress disorder, an anxiety disorder that can occur after experiencing a horrific event, such as war. Bocanegra is just one of many Iraq war veterans who have been prescribed the drugs from Veterans Affairs (VA) hospitals. He says that many VA hospitals are "putting a Band-Aid on a very big wound" by pre-scribing drugs to Iraq war veterans with mental problems.

the U.S. population. People with bipolar disorder have mood swings that often are extreme. When a person is feeling "up," or **manic**, he or she has increased energy and racing thoughts, feels elated, and may demonstrate poor judgment or take inappropriate risks. These manic periods alternate with periods during which the person feels "down." During these times, the person has symptoms associated with depression.

Although bipolar disorder and depression feature many of the same symptoms, the treatments are different. Depression often is treated with antidepressant medications, such as Prozac. It can be dangerous for people with bipolar disorder to take antidepressants because these drugs can make the manic periods worse. Bipolar disorder usually is treated with mood-stabilizing medications, such as **lithium**.

Seasonal Affective Disorder

A lot of people notice that they feel a bit "blue" during the fall and winter, as the days get shorter. Some people, however, become depressed at this time of year. In some cases, people experience problems in their work and relationships. This form of depression is known as **seasonal affective disorder**, or SAD. It affects more than 10 million Americans. A much rarer form of SAD, known as summer depression, happens in the warmer months. But the vast majority of SAD sufferers experience symptoms in the fall and winter.

People with SAD have the same blue and hopeless feelings that are seen in people with depression. They also need more sleep than usual and sometimes crave sweets or high-carbohydrate foods. This often leads to weight gain. People with SAD begin to experience symptoms of depression in the fall. Symptoms reach a peak in the winter. People slowly begin to feel better as spring arrives and the days get longer. Scientists believe that the lack of light in the winter causes the symptoms of SAD. Many doctors treat the condition with special light boxes.

Postpartum Depression

Dramatic changes in **hormone** levels during and after pregnancy can bring on depression. The most common form of pregnancy-related depression is **postpartum depression**, or PPD. This can occur at any time within a year after a woman gives birth. When a woman gets pregnant, her body begins to produce more estrogen and progesterone. Within the first 24 hours after child-birth, the levels of these hormones drop rapidly. These changes in hormone levels after pregnancy can trigger depression. In a similar way, changing hormone levels during a woman's menstrual cycle can cause mood swings. This is part of premenstrual syndrome, or PMS.

Women with postpartum depression may feel anxious, guilty, worthless, and sad. They have little energy and trouble concentrating. A woman with PPD may not be interested in caring for or spending time with her baby.

WHO GETS DEPRESSION?

Major depression affects between 15 million and 35 million Americans every year. The exact number of people affected is difficult to pinpoint. Many depressed people never seek treatment.

More than half of people who experience one depressive episode will go on to have future episodes, sometimes as often as once or twice each year. About half of all depressed people have their first episode between the ages of 20 and 50. Usually, people experience their first bout of depression at around age 40.

Depression affects people of all races, ethnicities, and socioeconomic classes. Women are twice as likely as men to become depressed. Older people also are more susceptible to depression. Around 6 million elderly people suffer from late-life depression. But only about 1 in 10 receives treatment. Depression affects young people, too. About 1 in 33 children and 1 in 8 teens suffer from major depression.

Depression often occurs with other illnesses. For example, up to 75% of people with eating disorders (such as **anorexia nervosa** and **bulimia**) also suffer from depression. Some 25% of cancer patients and 27% of people who abuse drugs and alcohol also are depressed. Depression does not only occur with other conditions; it also may play a role in *causing* certain physical ailments. A 1998 national report found that depressed people who have heart disease are four times more likely to have a heart attack, compared with people who have no history of depression.

THE COST OF DEPRESSION

At some point in their lives, more than 16% of Americans will suffer from a depression serious enough to need treatment. Unfortunately, most of them will never get the treatment they need. Two out of every three depressed people don't seek treatment. Many people are embarrassed or ashamed. They feel that there is a **stigma** attached to depression. As a result of this refusal to get help, depression is the leading cause of suicide. Suicide is the eleventh leading cause of death in the United States.

Depression has other tremendous costs to society. It is one of the top three problems on the job. Only family crises and stress cause more lost workdays, distraction, and other troubles. Each year, depression costs businesses in the United States around $70 billion in lost productivity and medical expenses.

Despite these high costs, the United States spends very little money on depression treatment. For each American, the United States spends $203 on cancer treatment and prevention and $1,000 on muscular dystrophy. But the United States spends only $10 per person to treat depression and related illnesses. Depression is very treatable. Experts estimate that more than 80% of cases can be successfully treated with medication, talk therapy, or both.

2

History of Antidepressants

Since ancient times, people have reported feeling the symptoms of depression. And for as long as these reports have been made, people have come up with different treatments.

ANCIENT REMEDIES

Plant products were among the earliest—and most successful—treatments for depression. For thousands of years, people have used extracts of the poppy plant (opium), St. John's wort (*Hypericum perforatum*), deadly nightshade (*Atropa belladonna*), and other plants to treat depression.

The ancient Sumerians called the poppy the "plant of joy" because people who consumed it felt happier and better about themselves. The poppy plant also

Medication made from the wildflower known as St. John's wort is widely considered a natural alternative to drugs in the treatment of depression, though it has recently been shown only to be effective in mild cases of depression. The plant's flowers and leaves are harvested and dried before being turned into a liquid or pill.

was commonly used as an antidepressant among the Minoans. They ruled the island of Crete (off the coast of Greece) during the third and second millennia B.C. Poppies were so popular for improving mood that they were traded widely among cultures around the Mediterranean Sea.

During the third millennium B.C., Assyrian records mention the use of deadly nightshade, or belladonna, to calm people and stabilize mood. In ancient Egypt, people used the henbane and thorn apple plants, along with alcohol, to ease feelings of melancholy. Over the years, these substances—especially alcohol—were widely used to change mood, and were often abused by people who enjoyed the way the substances made them feel.

Ancient cultures used a wide variety of plants to treat depression. They also recommended other forms of treatment. In both Greece and Egypt, a large part of medical treatment for mental health problems involved dancing, playing music, and sleeping in special temples that were supposed to cause healing dreams. Depressed people were entertained with plays or musical acts, put to work, or just generally distracted from thinking about their sad feelings. Sometimes the Greeks treated depression with massage and baths in special waters.

SELF-MEDICATING FOR DEPRESSION

Alcohol and other substances have long been used to treat depression and other mental illnesses. Many depressed people self-medicate by taking drugs or drinking alcohol. They use drugs and alcohol to relieve the pain, anxiety, **insomnia**, and other symptoms caused by their illness. As Will, a man who suffered from bipolar disorder, admitted in a post online, "I self-medicated with alcohol for more than 30 years and became addicted to prescription painkillers for about 10 years in a foolish attempt to gain enough control so that I could manage to keep working." About half of people with a mental illness also have a substance abuse problem. Unfortunately, the relief from self-medication doesn't last, and can cause many other problems.

DEPRESSION TREATMENT IN THE MIDDLE AGES

During the Middle Ages—from around the fourth century to the fifteenth century—the Christian Church
became the most powerful influence on people and society. Because of its great power, it had an impact on more
than just religion. It affected all aspects of life, including
medicine.

Early Christian churches and monasteries believed
that it was part of their duty to the community to take
care of people who suffered from mental illness. Over
time, however, magic and **mysticism** became influen-
tial. People believed that the minds of those with mental
disorders had been taken over by demons. Priests were
brought in to try to remove the evil spirits through
exorcisms or by scaring the demons with curses and
threats. Hospitals were still built to house people with
mental illness, but they became "madhouses" that were
more like dungeons. By the 1600s, people who had mental illnesses were often declared to be witches. Instead of
receiving treatment, they were tortured and killed.

Poor treatment was not universal, however. While
Europe was building madhouses to lock up the mentally
ill, Islamic countries treated people with mental illnesses much differently. By A.D. 765, a hospital devoted
exclusively to the treatment of mental illness had been
built in Baghdad, Iraq. Other hospitals—all of which
focused on the humane treatment of people with emotional and mood disorders—were also built in Cairo,
Egypt; Damascus, Syria; and Fez, Morocco. In these
places, people who suffered from depression and other
disorders received treatments to cheer them up and help
them see the positive side of life. People were exposed to
music, readings, and antidepressants, including caffeine,
opium, alcohol, and cannabis (marijuana).

DEPRESSION TREATMENT IN THE EIGHTEENTH AND NINETEENTH CENTURIES

By the 1700s, mentally ill people in Europe and America were seen as less than human. They were considered dangerous people who had to be locked away in order to protect the rest of society. The mentally ill were thrown into asylums. They lived in terrible conditions and received only the bare minimum of food, water, and care. Because of the dungeon-like rooms in which they were held, the poor diet, and the lack of fresh air, many people died in asylums.

Despite this horrendous treatment, attitudes about mental illness were gradually changing. Scientists were studying the nervous system. They were categorizing the different kinds of mental illness, which would allow them to study various disorders and try to find treatments. In 1793, a French doctor named Philippe Pinel suggested that treating people in mental asylums humanely might help them get better and perhaps return to their communities. Meanwhile, other doctors were working on medical treatments, including the same kinds of plants that had been in use since ancient times. Other cures also were attempted, including rest cures, bathing in special waters, and taking opium. It was not until the twentieth century that dramatic changes were made in the way mental illness was viewed and treated.

TREATING DEPRESSION IN THE TWENTIETH CENTURY

During the late nineteenth and early twentieth centuries, there was a gradual shift in how people thought about depression and other mental disorders. People began to think that mental illness was a biological problem that could be treated, or even cured, with medicine. At the

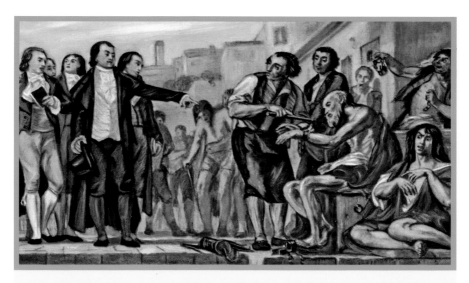

This painting shows French doctor Philippe Pinel removing chains from a mentally ill patient. Pinel helped pave the way for better treatment of the mentally ill in the late 1700s. His work enabled him to observe the mentally ill closely and compassionately and keep them out of dungeons, where they previously had been kept before.

same time, different forms of psychotherapy (talk therapy) became popular and were used to treat depression.

In the early 1900s, Austrian psychiatrist Sigmund Freud developed the theory of **psychoanalysis**. According to Freud, a person's mental illness could be traced to conflicts that had occurred when he or she was a child. Talking about and resolving those conflicts as an adult could relieve symptoms.

Freud's use of "talk therapy" laid the groundwork for other types of psychotherapy. Many of these are still popular, even though psychoanalysis fell out of favor in the late 20th century. Behavioral and cognitive therapies are two kinds that are still used today.

Scientists continued to look for biological causes for mental illnesses. They believed that if a physical cause could be found, then medicines also could be found that would help.

THE DEVELOPMENT OF MODERN ANTIDEPRESSANTS

By the 1950s, depression was widespread. Some scientists believed that finding a drug to treat depression would be as groundbreaking as the development of aspirin. Iproniazid was the first modern antidepressant. Just before its discovery, the best available antidepressant was opium. Opium is dangerously addictive.

TREATING DEPRESSION WITH SHOCK THERAPY

Electroshock therapy is formally known as electroconvulsive therapy, or ECT. Electricity was first used to treat patients in the sixteenth century, when electricity-producing fish, such as the black torpedo fish or electric ray, were used to help cure headaches. Using ECT to treat mental illness dates back to 1938. Developed by Italian researchers Lucio Bini and Ugo Cerletti, ECT uses an electric current to produce a seizure. This can help ease the symptoms of depression and other mental illnesses in certain cases in which the person has not responded to traditional antidepressants or talk therapy. Electrodes are attached to the person's skull. He or she is sedated so that the arms and legs won't thrash, which could result in broken bones or other injuries. ECT often looks violent in the movies, such as *One Flew Over the Cuckoo's Nest* (1975). Modern ECT is simple and usually done in a doctor's office.

Iproniazid was originally created to fight **tuberculosis**. Scientists found that it improved a person's mood and acted as a **stimulant**. Nathan Kline was a psychiatrist who studied the drug. Because it acted as a stimulant in people who were not depressed, Kline hoped it would act as an antidepressant in depressed people. Iproniazid was tested on 400,000 depressed people in 1957. More than 100 of them came down with **jaundice**. This severe side effect doomed the drug. It was never used as an antidepressant again.

At the same time, researcher Ronald Kuhn was trying to find an antidepressant drug that would not act

During the 1950s and 1960s, the first **psychotropic** drugs were being introduced. At this time, electroshock therapy stopped being used so much. The American Psychiatric Association set guidelines that said ECT could be used only for very serious cases of mental illness. In recent years, however, ECT has become more popular.

This is partly because some antidepressant drugs have been found to increase the risk of suicide, especially in young people. In England, these drugs have been banned. In the United States, the drugs now have labels that warn of the risk of suicide. As a result of this antidepressant scare, researchers have been studying ECT again. One study found that that ECT works as well as antidepressant drugs for moderate to severe cases of depression. Now, more physicians offer ECT as an option for treating depression.

Dr. Nathan Kline is remembered for his successful work with tranquilizers and antidepressants, which helped introduce a new era of psychiatry. Within a year of Kline's successful usage of iproniazid on patients suffering from depression, psychiatric centers across the country started giving patients antidepressants. A research institute in Orangeburg, NY, was named in his honor after his death in 1982.

as a stimulant. He was looking at **antihistamines**. In September 1957, he announced that he had come up with a new drug called imipramine. This was the first tricyclic antidepressant. Imipramine caused normal people to feel sedated. But it made depressed people feel better. However, imipramine affected many different parts of the body. It had a lot of side effects. The quest for a better antidepressant drug continued.

In the 1960s and 1970s, many scientists were studying the brain. They were trying to figure out what caused people to become depressed. As more was learned about the brain and how it worked, new antidepressants and other psychotropic drugs were created. These included Valium and Librium. Many of these drugs were addictive, though.

Trazodone was developed in the 1980s. It did help with depression. But trazodone also caused severe side effects, including sedation, tiredness, and dizziness. Because of these side effects, trazodone began to be used more often to treat anxiety than depression. As author Peter D. Kramer writes in *Listening to Prozac*, "This was the stage onto which Prozac walked: thirty years of **stasis** [i.e., a period of no change]."

3

Prozac

During the 1950s and 1960s, mental health research-ers were actively seeking new and better drugs to treat depression. They found a few drugs that worked against depression. All of the drugs, however, had serious side effects. By the late 1980s, a new drug had been created: Prozac.

THE HISTORY OF PROZAC

The history of the development of Prozac may have begun in 1953. That year, a British researcher named John Gaddum suggested that serotonin was important in "keeping us sane." Serotonin is one of the main neuro-transmitters in the brain. Because serotonin seemed to help improve mood, Gaddum thought that giving the brain more serotonin would help keep people from becoming depressed. His theory was supported by work done in 1963. Alec Coppen showed that depression could be helped by chemicals that worked the same way serotonin did. By the late 1960s, most scientists were convinced that serotonin did control mood and energy level. Researchers were trying to find a way to increase the amount of serotonin in the brain. Prozac would become the first drug to do this. It was the first of a group of drugs called selective serotonin reuptake inhibitors, or SSRIs.

By the 1970s, American pharmaceutical company Eli Lilly was working on developing an SSRI antidepressant. Led by Ray Fuller and David Wong, a special serotonin/depression research team began to test a new substance that would eventually become Prozac. In 1974, they began testing an early product that they called "Lilly 110140" or fluoxetine. Fluoxetine later became the generic name for Prozac. In 1976, the team tested Lilly 110140 on healthy volunteers. They found that it did not cause serious side effects. The company then recruited some famous psychiatrists to test the drug. The research showed that fluoxetine worked just as well as older tricyclic antidepressants. It also had very few side effects.

Additional tests of fluoxetine were done between 1984 and 1987. The results were very encouraging. People who tried the new drug felt happier and "wired." Tricyclic antidepressants had made them feel sluggish. Those drugs also often made them constipated. Prozac was approved to treat depression in Belgium in 1986. In December 1987, the Food and Drug Administration (FDA) approved Prozac for use in the United States. Since then, more than 90 other countries have approved the drug and more than 54 million people have taken it.

Prozac was almost immediately accepted as the perfect antidepressant drug. In March 1990, *Newsweek* did a cover story about it. The story talked about how popular Prozac was. It mentioned that the drug was helping to reduce the stigma of mental illness. "As Prozac's success stories mount, so does the sense that depression and other mental disorders are just that—treatable illnesses, not failings of character," the story said. Depression became something that people almost *wanted* to have. A doctor at Beth Israel Medical Center

PROZAC IN AMERICAN CULTURE

Prozac became the most widely prescribed psychiatric drug in the 1990s. Many celebrities began to publicly admit to taking it. In the past, famous people often tried to hide their depression. But the pop culture view of Prozac made it seem almost "cool" to be depressed.

Prozac was featured in music, movies, and books. The drug was featured in the names of the bands Prozac Ruin (punk rock) and Housewives on Prozac (rock). Journalist Elizabeth Wurtzel wrote a 1994 bestseller called *Prozac Nation*. In it, she talked about her own battle with depression.

In May 2005, actor Tom Cruise said that he believed antidepressants were dangerous. He made his statement after actress (and former co-star) Brooke Shields had praised antidepressants for helping her overcome post-partum depression. The public feud between Cruise and Shields brought even more attention to Prozac and its fellow antidepressants.

in New York City said, "Our phone rings off the hook every time someone does a story about Prozac. People want to try it. If you tell them they're not depressed, they say, 'Sure I am!'"

As Peter Kramer writes in *Listening to Prozac*, "Prozac enjoyed the fastest acceptance of any psychotherapeutic medicine—650,000 prescriptions per month by the time the *Newsweek* cover appeared [March 26, 1990], just over two years after Prozac was introduced." Also in 1990, researchers suggested that Prozac might be

Princeton-educated actress and former Calvin Klein model Brooke Shields suffered from postpartum depression following the birth of her first daughter, Rowan Francis, in 2003. In her 2005 book *Down Came the Rain*, Shields discussed the experience of living with deep depression, suicidal thoughts, and horrible images of someone harming her baby. She was able to recover with the help of antidepressant medication.

useful in treating other mental illnesses, such as panic and anxiety disorders, obsessive-compulsive disorder (OCD), premenstrual syndrome (PMS), substance abuse, and attention-deficit/hyperactivity disorder (ADHD). This further increased the number of people taking Prozac. Just three years after it was introduced, Prozac had become the most-prescribed drug in psychiatry.

OTHER ILLNESSES TREATED WITH PROZAC

Prozac became popular very quickly. Part of the reason was because it helps treat several conditions. These include:

- Alcoholism
- Borderline personality disorder, a condition that often affects young women and is characterized by unstable moods, problems with self-image, and impulsive behavior
- Sleep disorders, such as insomnia
- Post-traumatic stress disorder, an anxiety disorder that affects people who have been through a traumatic experience
- Phobias, or fears of specific objects or experiences
- Obsessive-compulsive disorder (OCD), an anxiety disorder that involves recurrent thoughts and/or repetitive behaviors
- Tourette syndrome, a disorder in which the person makes repeated sounds or movements (tics). The person cannot control the movements and sounds.
- Attention-deficit/hyperactivity disorder (ADHD), a condition that affects attention span and behavior

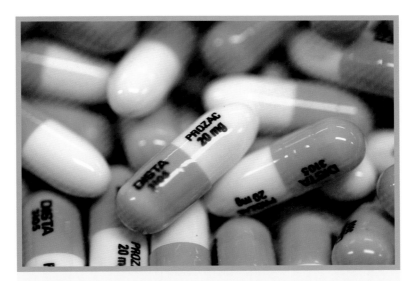

Prozac has been the subject of hundreds of lawsuits, including a 2002 case in which a Tennessee woman claimed the drug caused her husband to hang himself 13 days after his cardiologist prescribed Prozac for his chest pain and weight loss.

HOW PROZAC WORKS

It's thought that people with depression don't have enough serotonin, a neurotransmitter that affects mood. Many nerve cells use serotonin to send signals to one another. The serotonin is released by one neuron, travels across a synapse, and attaches to another neuron. This produces a signal in the second neuron. After a signal is sent, some of the serotonin is broken down. But most of it is recycled. An uptake pump absorbs the leftover serotonin (this is called **reuptake**). Prozac blocks this pump, so serotonin builds up in the synapse. The next time the same neuron sends a message, there will be more serotonin in the synapse and the signal will be stronger. Prozac lets a person's neurons "soak" in serotonin for a longer time than they would without the drug.

Prozac comes in several forms: a tablet, a capsule, a liquid, and in a delayed-release form. Normally, Prozac is taken by mouth once or twice a day. The delayed-release form is taken only once a week.

Prozac does not start working right away. It takes several weeks for the drug to build up in the bloodstream and start affecting serotonin.

POSSIBLE SIDE EFFECTS

Many studies have been done on Prozac's side effects. Compared with most other antidepressant drugs, Prozac has few side effects.

Some Prozac users are allergic to the drug. They get skin rashes or redness. Some people get headaches, dizziness, tremors, and a feeling of weakness. Other people may feel tired, agitated, nervous, or anxious. Some people have trouble sleeping. Others sweat a lot.

Gastrointestinal side effects include diarrhea, changes in appetite, and nausea. Some people lose weight. This is an unusual side effect for an antidepressant. Most antidepressants can cause weight gain. Before Prozac was approved to treat depression, researchers thought about testing it as a weight-loss drug.

Prozac can cause other side effects. These include sore throat or soreness in the **mucous membranes** in the nose. Prozac makes some people yawn a lot. Some people get **bronchitis**. Muscle and bone pain also occur in some people. Some women have painful menstrual periods while on Prozac. Some people may get urinary tract infections. Other side effects include:

- Dry mouth
- Water retention (bloating)
- Constipation
- Restlessness

- Sedation
- Weakness
- Fever
- Swelling of the face, hands, feet, ankles, or lower legs
- Problems breathing or swallowing
- Seizures

The side effects usually go away within a few weeks after a person starts taking Prozac. If they don't go away, they often aren't serious enough to bother people. If side effects do start to bother a person, they can be treated with other medicines. Rarely, the side effects are bad enough that the person has to stop taking Prozac and try another drug.

PROBLEMS WITH PROZAC

Prozac is considered a wonder drug and a life saver. Yet, over the past few years, researchers have found that some antidepressants—including Prozac—may increase the risk of suicide in a small number of people. It isn't entirely clear why this happens. However, about 1 in every 100 people who take Prozac developed a form of anxiety called **akathisia**. This causes them to try to kill themselves. Other people appear to commit suicide because taking an antidepressant like Prozac gives them back some of the energy that their depression has been sapping, giving them the ability to overcome the desire to do nothing and use it to kill themselves. Because of the risk of suicide as a result of these and other causes, Prozac labels must now carry a warning that lets users know about the risk of suicide.

4

Tricyclic Antidepressants

Tricyclic antidepressants were discovered by accident during the 1950s. Scientists were trying to develop a new drug to treat **schizophrenia**—the mental disorder in which people see and hear things that are not actually there and believe things that are not true. They found that a drug called imipramine was actually better at treating depression. Imipramine was sold under the brand name Tofranil. It worked in about 60% of patients. From the 1960s until the late 1980s, when Prozac was introduced, tricyclics were the first choice for treating depression. Even today, they are often more effective than other antidepressants for severe depression. This is especially true in people who have tried other drugs, but found they didn't help. Tricyclic drugs are good for treating depression that is caused by chemical or hormonal changes.

WHAT ARE TRICYCLICS?

Tricyclics got their name from their molecular three-ring shape. They are made of two **benzene** rings connected by another ring that contains nitrogen, oxygen, or carbon.

After the relative success of Tofranil (imipramine), other tricyclic antidepressants were developed. They include:

- Amitriptyline (brand name Elavil or Endep)
- Clominpramine (brand name Anafranil)
- Doxepin (brand name Sinequan or Adapin)
- Desipramine (brand name Norpramin)
- Nortriptyline (brand name Pamelor)
- Protriptyline (brand name Vivactil)
- Trimipramine (brand name Surmontil)

Tricyclic antidepressants work on two neurotransmitters: norepinephrine and serotonin. There are two broad types of tricyclics. One is called the tertiary amines. This group includes amitriptyline, imipramine, trimipramine, and doxeprin. These drugs tend to increase levels of serotonin more than norepinephrine. They can make people feel sedated. The second group is called the secondary amines. These drugs tend to boost levels of norepinephrine more than serotonin. This can make people feel agitated.

Tricyclic antidepressants are taken once a day. They usually come in pill form. They also come in liquid and injectable forms. The amount each person should take depends on many things. These include age, weight, general health, and the type of depression that is being treated. Like Prozac, tricyclics normally take two to four weeks to work. A doctor usually starts a person on a low dose. Gradually, he or she works up to a larger dose. The doctor keeps track of how well the drug is working. Tricyclics may continue to work for up to a week after a person stops taking them.

HOW TRICYCLICS WORK

Like Prozac, tricyclic antidepressants work by changing the way neurotransmitters are used in the brain.

ARE TRICYCLIC ANTIDEPRESSANTS A RISK FACTOR FOR EPILEPSY?

In April 2000, a study was presented at the American Epilepsy Society's annual meeting. It was conducted by researchers in both the United States and Iceland and led by W. Allen Hauser. The study found that having depression may make people more likely to develop epilepsy. The study also found that taking tricyclic antidepressants may increase this risk even more.

Over three years, the researchers looked at new cases of epilepsy. They found that these people also tended to have depression. People who took tricyclics had triple the risk of epilepsy, compared with people who took other types of antidepressants. The risk was even higher in people under the age of 55.

The researchers don't know why people who take tricyclics are more likely to get epilepsy. They are still looking into it. They are also studying other antidepressant drugs to see if there are other links with epilepsy.

Tricyclics increase the amounts of norepinephrine and serotonin. Both of these are involved in the regulation of moods and feeling stressed.

Different tricyclics tend to affect different symptoms. Tertiary tricyclics may cause sedation. Secondary tricyclics can cause agitation. A person with depression who is restless and agitated would benefit more from a tertiary tricyclic. Someone who feels sluggish because of depression would likely do better taking a secondary tricyclic.

Tricyclics often are effective. But they can have many side effects. This is most likely because tricyclics affect

USING TRICYCLICS TO TREAT LONG-TERM PAIN

Some tricyclic antidepressants are excellent choices for treating long-term pain. Amitriptyline is the tricyclic that is used most often to treat pain. Others—including imipramine, desipramine, and nortriptyline—also work as painkillers.

It isn't clear why these tricyclics relieve pain. Scientists believe that they may work by increasing the amount of neurotransmitters that reduce pain in the spinal cord. This can reduce the number of pain signals being sent through the body. Although it can take several weeks to feel the effects, tricyclic antidepressants can be very good at treating the burning, searing types of pain that often occur with **diabetes**, strokes, **shingles**, or nerve damage. Tricyclics may also be good for treating **fibromyalgia** and for preventing **migraines**.

other transmitters besides norepinephrine and sero-tonin. Histamine is one of these. Histamine plays a role in regulating the immune system. Acetylcholine, which affects mood and muscle movement, is also affected by tricyclics.

SIDE EFFECTS OF TRICYCLICS

One reason why tricyclics are no longer the most popu-lar form of antidepressant drugs is that they tend to produce many side effects. Some of the most common ones include:

- Blurred vision
- Lightheadedness
- Sedation or drowsiness
- Trouble sleeping
- Sweating
- Weight gain
- Appetite changes or nausea
- Confusion
- Rapid heartbeat
- Dry mouth
- Constipation
- Skin rashes
- Tremors
- Seizures
- Low blood pressure
- Sensitivity to sunlight
- Weakness

Tricyclic antidepressants also may interact with other medicines. Sometimes the results can be dangerous. This is true when tricyclics are mixed with **anesthetic** medications that are given during surgeries and some dental procedures and emergency medical treatments.

Tricyclics also can change the results of medical tests. This makes it complicated and confusing for doctors trying to treat other disorders. Tricyclics, for example, may affect blood sugar levels, which can make it difficult to treat conditions such as diabetes. They also can interfere with how other drugs work. Anyone who takes a tricyclic antidepressant should let his or her doctors know about all the other medicines they take.

5

Selective Serotonin Reuptake Inhibitors (SSRIs)

Selective serotonin reuptake inhibitors (SSRIs) were discovered in the late 1980s. They continued to be developed through the 1990s. Older antidepressants, including the tricyclics and monoamine oxidase inhibitors, caused so many side effects that they were often dangerous to use. Researchers wanted to create drugs that would affect only serotonin and not other neurotransmitters. They thought this strategy would treat depression without causing many of the common side effects of other antidepressants. In other words, researchers were looking for a drug that was "selective" in acting on serotonin. This is where the name *selective serotonin reuptake inhibitor* comes from.

THE HISTORY OF SSRIs

The first SSRI was Prozac (its generic name is fluoxetine). Introduced in 1987, Prozac quickly became the most commonly prescribed antidepressant. Drug companies scrambled to produce other SSRIs. SSRIs seem to be especially good at stopping depression in its early stages, before it becomes severe.

Through the 1990s, a slew of new SSRIs was developed. SSRIs rapidly became one of the most widely prescribed classes of drugs in the world. They virtually eliminated the market for older antidepressants, including tricyclics. Today, SSRIs make up 81% of the antidepressant market.

As SSRIs became more popular, attitudes toward depression and other mental health problems changed dramatically. People became less ashamed of having depression. Many people started to think that depression was a disease, rather than a personality problem. Many people started visiting their regular (primary care) doctors for depression treatment, rather than seeking the help of psychiatrists. In the past, psychiatrists treated almost all cases of depression. In part, primary care doctors could safely prescribe SSRIs because they had so few side effects. Today, primary care doctors prescribe 81% of the antidepressants in this country. Sixty percent of people visiting a doctor are diagnosed with mental health issues, rather than with physical disorders.

Some writers believe that drug companies have actually promoted depression to sell more drugs. Drug companies market antidepressants to primary care doctors. They also advertise directly to Americans through television ads. Some think that all of this advertising makes depression seem more widespread than it really is. According to *The Economist*, there are approximately

50,000 to 100,000 people with depression per million people worldwide. That makes depression more common than AIDS or heart disease. But before SSRIs were developed, depression was believed to affect only 100 people out of every million.

WHICH DRUGS ARE SSRIs?

The SSRIs are:

- Fluoxetine (brand name Prozac)
- Citalopram (brand name Celexa)
- Escitalopram (brand name Lexapro)
- Paroxetine (brand name Paxil)
- Sertraline (brand name Zoloft)
- Fluvoxamine (brand name Luvox)

SSRIs have different pros and cons. Prozac tends to act as a mild stimulant. It's better, then, for people who feel sluggish or have little energy. Prozac also stays in the body longer than the other SSRIs. In some cases, the drug is still in the bloodstream six weeks after a person has stopped taking it. Paroxetine, on the other hand, has a **half-life** of only about 21 hours, so it exits the body fairly quickly. Paroxetine tends to act like a sedative. It may cause constipation. Sertraline has a half-life of around 26 hours. It does not act like a stimulant or a sedative. It may cause diarrhea.

HOW SSRIs WORK

All SSRIs work by making more serotonin available in the brain. They are good at treating both **acute** and long-term depression. Certain SSRIs, including Prozac, also can prevent new episodes of depression. A person has to take an SSRI for two to six weeks before seeing improvement.

Fine-tuning an anti-depressant

The anti-depressant "selective serotonin re-uptake inhibitors", SSRIs, blocks the reabsorption of serotonin – a messenger chemical that is known to influence many of the brain's functions including sleep, appetite and mood.

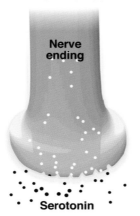

Nerve ending

Serotonin

A brain cell emits serotonin. Some serotonin is absorbed by other brain cells, some is reabsorbed by the sending cell.

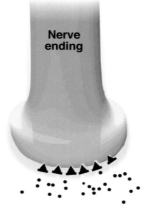

Nerve ending

SSRIs block the reabsorption of serotonin. The higher levels of serotonin increase brain cell stimulation.

SOURCE: Associated Press

AP

This image helps illustrate how SSRIs block serotonin from being reabsorbed by the brain cells from which they are released. This allows serotonin to be absorbed by other brain cells, resulting in increased brain cell stimulation. In the second image, the SSRIs are shown as dark triangles that block the serotonin from coming back into their original cells.

SSRIs are some of the safest antidepressants. They don't often cause unpleasant or dangerous side effects. But they are expensive. SSRIs usually are taken once a day as a pill. Each pill costs $2 to $3. If a person's health insurance plan doesn't cover the SSRI, he or she may not be able to afford it.

Besides depression, SSRIs can help in treating panic attacks, post-traumatic stress disorder, obsessive-compulsive disorder, and social anxiety disorder.

SIDE EFFECTS OF SSRIs

It's true that SSRIs cause fewer side effects and are less dangerous than older types of antidepressants. That does not mean that SSRIs cause no side effects at all. In some cases, the side effects caused by SSRIs can be as bad as those caused by other drugs.

SSRIs are not the best choice for every person. People who have kidney or liver disease usually avoid them.

DO SSRIs REDUCE THE RISK OF COLON CANCER?

A 2006 study published in the April issue of *Lancet Oncology* said that SSRIs might prevent colon cancer, or at least slow its growth.

The study involved 3,367 people and lasted almost 20 years. The results showed that people who had taken an SSRI were less likely to be diagnosed with colon cancer. The researchers also said that taking tricyclics slightly increased the risk of colon cancer.

Animal studies have shown that serotonin might have something to do with the growth of colon cancer. Past studies also found that SSRIs slow down cancer growth in mice, and slow the division of cancer cells in rats.

Their conditions can cause high levels of SSRIs to build up in their bodies. SSRIs also can make mania worse, so they usually are not given to people with mania.

Early in the course of treatment, SSRIs may make people more nervous or anxious. This anxiety often goes away after a few weeks. But some people stay so anxious that they have to stop taking the drug. SSRIs also can cause indigestion and nausea.

Other side effects include:

- Loss of appetite
- Increased appetite and weight gain
- Allergies
- Dry mouth
- Headache
- Irritability
- Drowsiness
- Shaking
- Dizziness
- Convulsions
- Sweating
- Bruising
- Diarrhea
- Low levels of sodium
- Problems sleeping
- Weakness
- Reduced sexual drive

SSRIs also can lead to a condition called serotonin syndrome. This is rare, but it can be life threatening. It usually happens when a person takes an SSRI while he or she also is taking a monoamine oxidase inhibitor (MAOI) antidepressant or certain other medicines or diet supplements, including St. John's wort. In serotonin syndrome, the brain becomes overloaded with serotonin. Symptoms include:

- Restlessness
- Agitation
- Changes in blood pressure

DO SSRIs LEAD TO THE RISK OF FRACTURES?

In older people, taking an SSRI may increase the risk of breaking a bone after a fall. A study led by Dr. David Goltzman of McGill University in Montreal looked at bone density measurements of 137 people. Their average age was 65. All were taking SSRIs. After five years, the risk of broken bones had doubled. People in the study were especially likely to suffer breaks in the bones of the forearm, foot, and ankle. According to the report, taking an SSRI decreased bone density by about 4% in the hip and 2.5% in the spine. Goltzman said, "There is good scientific evidence that serotonin is involved in bone physiology, and if you alter the system, you get low bone density." Some scientists have challenged the findings, saying that the study only looked at people who were taking antidepressants, not people of the same age who were not on such medications, so the data discovered may not be entirely accurate. Some medical professionals also worry that studies like this one will discourage people who need SSRIs from taking them. In the future, scientists will do more work to see if SSRIs affect bone density. They will compare people who take SSRIs with people who take other antidepressants.

- Confusion
- Hallucinations
- Rapid heart rate
- Seizures
- Fever
- Nausea and vomiting
- Coma

If someone who is taking an SSRI has any of these symptoms, he or she needs to see a doctor right away. People who stop taking an MAOI should wait at least two weeks before they start taking an SSRI.

SSRIs also can interact with other medicines and even some foods. Tryptophan is an amino acid found in several foods, including turkey. The combination of tryptophan and an SSRI can cause nausea, sweating, dizziness, and headache. If a person is given warfarin (an anti-clotting drug) while taking Paxil, he or she may find that cuts or scrapes won't stop bleeding. SSRIs can cause gas and nausea or even seizures when mixed with alcohol, although having seizures is rare.

When people stop taking SSRIs, they do so by gradually reducing the amount they take over time. If they just suddenly stop taking an SSRI, they can get headaches or flu-like symptoms. Some people get dizzy or feel sluggish.

THE RISK OF SUICIDE AND SSRIs

In 2006, the FDA decided that warning labels should be placed on SSRIs. The labels say that some people will be more likely to have suicidal thoughts and attempt suicide while taking the drugs. This is especially true for people between the ages of 18 and 24. But in people over the age of 65, SSRIs appear to *decrease* the risk of suicide. The suicide risk is most likely to happen in the early weeks of treatment. Because of this risk, SSRIs are no longer used to treat depression in children and adolescents. The exception is Prozac. It still is used to treat major depressive disorder in young people. Also, other SSRIs are still used to treat other problems in young people, such as obsessive-compulsive disorder.

6

Monoamine Oxidase Inhibitors (MAOIs)

Just as the first group pf antidepressants—tricyclics—was discovered by chance, so was the second group. They are called monoamine oxidase inhibitors, or MAOIs.

Iproniazid was the first modern antidepressant. It was discovered in the early 1950s. A scientist named E. A. Zeller found that iproniazid slowed the breakdown of three neurotransmitters: serotonin, dopamine, and norepinephrine. These three chemicals are broken down by an **enzyme** called monoamine oxidase. Iproniazid makes this enzyme work more slowly, allowing more of the monoamine neurotransmitters to stay in the brain longer. Because they block the enzyme monoamine oxidase, iproniazid and related drugs became known as monoamine oxidase inhibitors. These drugs were identified as antidepressants in the early 1950s. But it took almost a decade before they began to be used to treat depressed people. MAOIs are usually not the preferred treatment for depression, though. They cause many side effects. Some are serious, and some can be fatal. Still, MAOIs are used to treat depression when other drugs don't help.

HOW MAOIs WORK

MAOIs stop the enzyme monoamine oxidase from destroying three neurotransmitters: serotonin, norepinephrine, and dopamine. When a message is sent in the brain, these neurotransmitters are used as chemical signals. Once the message has been sent, monoamine oxidase tries to "clean up" the extra neurotransmitters. MAOIs stop this from happening. This leaves more neurotransmitters in the brain, which improves mood and relieves depression.

The monoamine oxidase enzyme comes in different forms. There are high levels of the enzyme in the brain and liver. It also is found in the stomach, intestinal wall, and kidneys. There are two forms: MAO-A and MAO-B. MAO-A is found mainly in the stomach and intestines. MAO-B is found mainly in the brain. MAO-A breaks down certain chemicals in foods.

Monoamine oxidase doesn't just burn up serotonin, norepinephrine, and dopamine. It also destroys tyramine. This chemical helps control blood pressure. Tyramine can be very dangerous if it builds up in the brain. The blood pressure in the brain can get so high that blood vessels begin to burst. This can be fatal. To prevent this from happening, people who take MAOIs need to be very careful to avoid consuming foods or drinks that contain tyramine, in order to keep levels of this chemical as low as possible.

The FDA has approved several MAOIs to treat depression. They include:

- Phenelzine (brand name Nardil)
- Tranylcypromine (brand name Parnate)
- Isocarboxazid (brand name Marplan)
- Moclobemide (brand name Manerix; this drug is not available in the United States)
- Selegiline (brand name Emsam)

USING MAOIs TO TREAT SOCIAL ANXIETY DISORDER

People who suffer from social anxiety disorder may just seem shy. But the condition is more serious than shyness. People with social anxiety become very anxious when they believe they might be embarrassed. This could be at a large party, a small get-together, or any social situation. This disorder usually develops during childhood or the teen years. It can last for a lifetime. It is the third most common psychological disorder, after depression and alcohol abuse.

Studies have shown that certain MAOIs, particularly phenelzine (Nardil), are effective in treating the symptoms of social anxiety disorder. In fact, Nardil is believed to be the most effective antidepressant of any type to treat this condition. However, the FDA's approval of Emsam in 2006 has raised the hopes of scientists who study social anxiety disorder. Emsam has fewer health risks than other MAOIs. Research is still going on, but many people believe Emsam may work just as well as Nardil in relieving social anxiety.

MAOIs are usually taken as pills. But the most recent member of the MAOI family, Emsam, is given through a patch that is placed on the skin. The FDA approved Emsam in February 2006. A person places a new patch on his or her upper arm, thigh, or torso every day. Researchers believe that delivering an MAOI through the skin may be less risky. The drug is absorbed directly into the blood. It does not go through the stomach and intestines. This way, people can take lower doses of the drug and still get the same effects. This may make Emsam safer than other MAOIs. People may be able to eat more of a normal diet, without worrying about how much tyramine they eat.

FOODS TO AVOID WHILE TAKING MAOIs

The amino acid tyramine is found in many foods. MAOIs increase a person's levels of tyramine. High levels of tyramine can be dangerous and even fatal. So people who take MAOIs should be very careful about what they eat and drink. Some of the foods and beverages that people who take MAOIs should be careful about are listed below.

FOODS TO AVOID

Most alcoholic beverages, especially red wine
Bean curd
Fava beans
Cheese
Fish
Ginseng
Products made with proteins
Liver

WHO SHOULD AND SHOULDN'T TAKE MAOIs

MAOIs are used most often to treat **atypical depression**. People with this disease sleep and eat too much and take other people's comments very personally, getting more upset than the average person would. They also have strong reactions to the environment, such as heightened sensitivity to light and noise. People with atypical depression also tend to have anxiety. They may have phobias or be **hypochondriacs**. People with atypical depression also may not seem to care about anything or be interested in anything. Phenelzine (Nardil) has helped many people with this type of depression.

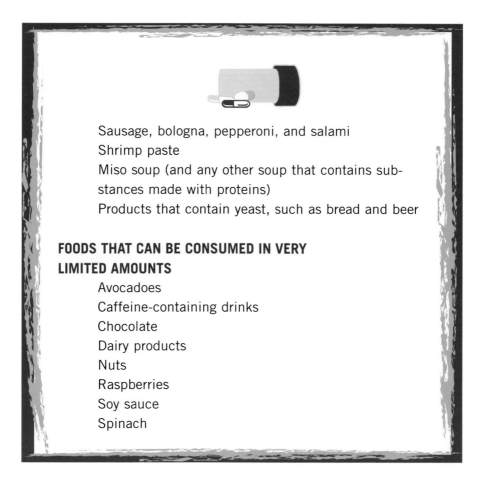

Sausage, bologna, pepperoni, and salami
Shrimp paste
Miso soup (and any other soup that contains substances made with proteins)
Products that contain yeast, such as bread and beer

FOODS THAT CAN BE CONSUMED IN VERY LIMITED AMOUNTS
Avocadoes
Caffeine-containing drinks
Chocolate
Dairy products
Nuts
Raspberries
Soy sauce
Spinach

MAOIs can work wonders for people with atypical depression. But many people need to avoid these drugs. Among them are people with high blood pressure, heart conditions, epilepsy, asthma, or bronchitis. Some of the MAOIs may also cause agitation. People whose depression includes symptoms of restlessness should generally not take an MAOI.

SIDE EFFECTS OF MAOIs

MAOIs produce many dangerous side effects. They are rarely used today. They can be prescribed for people who have tried other types of antidepressants but haven't gotten relief from their symptoms.

The best-known side effects seen with MAOIs are dietary. MAOIs are known to produce something called the "cheese effect" or "cheese reaction." This is a set of symptoms that tend to happen when a person eats certain foods, such as aged cheeses and red wines. These foods have high levels of tyramine. The symptoms include a sudden spike in blood pressure, a severe headache in the front of the head, a sore or stiff neck, chest pain, heart palpitations, nausea or vomiting, sweating, sensitivity to light, and dilated pupils. If any of these symptoms occur while a person is taking MAOIs, he or she should see a doctor or go to an emergency room. The rise in blood pressure can cause bleeding in the brain, as well as heart problems.

The other side effects that MAOIs produce can be unpleasant, but they are generally not deadly. They include:

- Headache
- Low blood pressure
- Drowsiness or sedation
- Diarrhea or upset stomach

- Blurred vision
- Changes in appetite
- Shakiness
- Weakness
- Dry mouth
- Fatigue
- Lightheadedness/fainting, especially when standing up quickly or getting up after lying down
- Chest pain
- Constipation

DRUGS TO AVOID WHILE TAKING MAOIs

MAOIs can cause dangerous interactions with many drugs. People who are considering taking an MAOI should talk with their doctors about the other drugs they are currently taking. Aspirin, plain Tylenol, Motrin, and antibiotics are safe to take while on an MAOI. Still, people should check with their doctors or pharmacists before taking any other drug. The following drugs are among those that are the most dangerous to mix with other drugs:

- Allergy medicines
- Appetite suppressants
- Asthma medicines
- Cold medicines
- Insulin
- Ritalin
- Sinus medicine
- Wellbutrin

- Sleep disturbances
- Changes in blood sugar level, especially in diabetics

MAOIs can also interact with other drugs, including other antidepressants, pain medicines such as tramadol, weight-loss products, and over-the-counter deconges-tants. Like tricyclic antidepressants, MAOIs can interfere with anesthesia drugs.

As mentioned previously, combining MAOIs with SSRIs and certain other antidepressants can result in serotonin syndrome. It is important to avoid taking an MAOI and an SSRI within at least two weeks of each other.

7

Other Antidepressants

Even after the astounding success of Prozac and its fellow SSRIs, scientists continued to look for newer and better drugs to treat depression. Some antidepressants seemed to help by increasing the amount of serotonin and/or norepinephrine in people's brains. Studies began looking at what would happen if the levels of other neurotransmitters were increased. This research led to a variety of new antidepressant drugs.

SEROTONIN AND NOREPINEPHRINE REUPTAKE INHIBITORS (SNRIs)

Scientists knew that MAOI antidepressants increased the amounts of serotonin and norepinephrine in the brain. The drawback is that MAOIs also affect tyramine. A safer and more effective drug would act only on serotonin and norepinephrine, leaving tyramine alone. This idea led to the development of serotonin and norepinephrine reuptake inhibitors (SNRIs). These drugs are sometimes known as dual reuptake inhibitors because they affect the reuptake of two neurotransmitters.

SNRIs ease the symptoms of depression by making more serotonin and norepinephrine available in the brain. Scientists still aren't exactly sure how SNRIs do this. One theory is that SNRIs increase the number of chemical messages that are sent in the brain.

The FDA has approved two SNRI drugs for treating depression: duloxetine (Cymbalta) and venlafaxine

USING SNRIs TO TREAT FIBROMYALGIA

Fibromyalgia is a long-term disease. It causes pain in muscles, tendons, and ligaments. It's also called chronic muscle pain syndrome or fibrositis. Fibromyalgia affects women more often than men. It is not life threatening, but it can be very uncomfortable. Fibromyalgia almost never goes away, even with treatment. Besides being in pain, people with fibromyalgia are exhausted. Different places on their bodies feel very tender, even to the slightest touch. In some cases, people with fibromyalgia experience symptoms of depression.

Although fibromyalgia cannot be cured, it can be treated. Some of the best drugs for treating are SNRIs, including Cymbalta and Effexor.

(Effexor). These drugs also are used to treat anxiety. Duloxetine also helps treat pain associated with diabetes. Serotonin and norepinephrine help the body handle pain. If more of these neurotransmitters are available, the body may do a better job at dealing with pain.

As with all antidepressants, SNRIs can cause side effects. The most common include:

- Nausea or vomiting
- Headache
- Insomnia
- Dry mouth
- Yawning or sleepiness
- Dizziness
- Constipation
- Sweating
- Anxiety
- Agitation
- Blurred or double vision
- Shakiness
- Strange dreams
- Gas
- High blood pressure

As with SSRIs, taking an SNRI with an MAOI can cause serotonin syndrome. People should avoid taking an SNRI and an MAOI within at least two weeks of one another.

TETRACYCLIC ANTIDEPRESSANTS

Tetracyclic antidepressants are related to tricyclic antidepressants. But tetracyclics have a four-ring chemical structure while tricyclics have a three-ring structure.

SSRIs, MAOIs, and SNRIs ease depression by reducing the reabsorption of neurotransmitters. Tetracyclics bind with parts of nerve cells in the brain called alpha-2 receptors. This binding somehow increases the amounts of serotonin and norepinephrine in the brain.

The FDA has approved one tetracyclic to treat depression. It is called mirtazapine (brand name Remeron). It can be taken as a pill or as a tablet that dissolves on the tongue (called Remeron SolTab).

Tetracyclics do not always cause side effects, but some people experience:

- Drowsiness
- Lightheadedness
- Muscle or joint pain
- Weight gain
- Dry mouth or thirst
- Constipation
- Changes in appetite
- Increased cholesterol levels
- Heart palpitations
- Sweating

Tetracyclic antidepressants can interact with certain other types of drugs. This can cause more serious side effects. If someone is taking a tricyclic and has any of the following side effects, he or she should see a doctor right away:

- Skin rashes
- Sore throat
- Changes in menstrual cycle
- Confusion
- Chills
- Problems breathing
- Fever

- Hallucinations
- Seizures

NOREPINEPHRINE AND DOPAMINE REUPTAKE INHIBITORS (NDRIs)

Norepinephrine and dopamine reuptake inhibitors (NDRIs) work just as their name suggests: They increase the levels of norepinephrine and dopamine in the brain. Scientists believe they work in two ways. They not only slow the reuptake of these two neurotransmitters, but also increase the number of chemical messages sent in the brain.

The FDA has approved one NDRI for the treatment of depression. It is called buproprion (brand name Wellbutrin.) (Another form of buproprion, called either Buproban or Zyban, has been approved to help people quit smoking.) Buproprion is available in a few different forms. It comes as an immediate-release formula that is taken three times a day. It also comes in a twice-a-day slow-release form, as well as an extended-release form, which needs to be taken just once a day.

Although side effects are generally mild, NDRIs can cause any of the following:

- Frequent urination
- Loss of appetite
- Sore throat
- Dry mouth
- Rapid heartbeat
- Skin rash
- Nausea or vomiting
- Muscle pain
- Sweating
- Stomach pain

- Anxiety
- Dizziness
- Ringing in the ears
- Constipation
- Nervousness or shakiness

USING ANTIDEPRESSANTS TO QUIT SMOKING

Like many drugs, Zyban—an NDRI that is used to help people quit smoking—was discovered by accident. Wellbutrin was first introduced in 1984 as an antidepressant. Some smokers had been prescribed Wellbutrin for depression. They noticed that it also seemed to make them crave cigarettes less than usual. The drug company that made Wellbutrin, GlaxoSmithKline, did some more testing. In 1997, the company introduced Zyban, an NDRI to help people stop smoking. Although the drug is chemically the same as Wellbutrin, GlaxoSmithKline chose to use the brand name Zyban for the drug when it is used to help people quit smoking.

Zyban (or Buproban) appears to work by reducing the withdrawal symptoms that people usually feel when they try to quit smoking, including anger, irritability, depression, trouble concentrating, and restlessness. It also reduces the urge to smoke, although scientists are not exactly sure how it does that.

Unlike most other products used to quit smoking, Zyban does not contain any nicotine. That means that the person using it can also use a nicotine patch, gum, or lozenge without running the risk of overdosing on

In some people, NDRIs can cause high blood pressure. NDRIs also can cause seizures. This happens mainly in people who have a history of seizures, and especially those who have had head injuries, brain tumors, or eating disorders. NDRIs also can be dangerous if taken with MAOIs.

Dr. Jasjit Ahluwalia of the Kansas University Medical Center in Kansas City, Kansas, holds the drug Zyban. Researchers at the University of Kansas have done studies to show how the anti-smoking pill also works as an antidepressant.

nicotine. Success rates for quitting smoking with Zyban have been reported as high as 58%. On average, though, between about 15% and 25% of smokers wind up quitting when they use Zyban.

COMBINED REUTAKE INHIBITORS AND RECEPTOR BLOCKERS

Combined reuptake inhibitors and receptor blockers are known as dual-action antidepressants. This means that they work in two different ways: by inhibiting the reabsorption of neurotransmitters and by blocking nerve cell receptors. Both actions make more neurotransmitters available in the brain.

The FDA has approved three of these drugs to treat depression. They are only available as generic drugs. They are trazodone, nefazodone, and maprotiline.

Combined reuptake inhibitors and receptor blockers have some side effects:

- Headache
- Dry mouth
- Confusion
- Dizziness
- Constipation
- Confusion
- Problems with vision
- Drowsiness
- Nervousness
- Nausea or vomiting
- Weakness
- Lightheadedness

Sometimes these drugs cause other side effects. Nefazodone, for example, has been known to cause liver failure. Anyone who takes nefazodone should become familiar with the signs of liver problems (dark urine, nausea or pain in the abdomen, a loss of appetite, and yellowing of the skin or whites of the eyes). They should seek medical help quickly if any of these signs appear. Maprotiline is associated with seizures, mainly in people who have already suffered from some form of seizure disorder in the past. Like many other antidepressants, this drug also can be dangerous when taken with an MAOI.

8

Alternative Treatments for Depression

For much of the twentieth century and into the twenty-first, antidepressant drugs have been viewed by many people as the best, most effective, and fastest treatment for depression. But many other therapies also can help treat depression.

TALK THERAPY

Sigmund Freud introduced his theories of psychoanalysis in the early twentieth century. Since then, encouraging patients to talk with a trained health-care professional has been viewed as one of the best ways to deal with mental health problems. Some people consider talk therapy to be better than the use of psychiatric drugs. According to Robert J. DeRubeis, chair of the psychology department at the University of Pennsylvania, "Psychotherapy has really been undersold as a treatment for depression. But [it] works just as well as medication, even in severely depressed people." Researchers from the University of Pennsylvania and Vanderbilt University compared the most common antidepressant drugs with one form of talk therapy (cognitive therapy). They found that people who used medication felt better sooner. But after four months, both groups had the same success rate. And in the long term, over the course of a year beyond the four-month check-in, the effects of talk therapy lasted longer. About 75% of the talk therapy patients still felt better after about a year and a half, compared with 60% of those who took medicine.

There are different forms of talk therapy. All share certain basic goals:

- Exploring the person's relationships and life experiences
- Setting goals
- Learning about the causes of the person's condition
- Identifying negative thoughts and behaviors, and changing them
- Learning new ways to deal with problems

Some people use talk therapy for only a few months or even a few weeks. They use it to deal with a specific issue. More often, though, a person continues to see his or her therapist for many months or years. This allows people to address problems and maintain their mental health over time.

Talk therapy is usually done with one person meeting with one counselor. However, in some cases, counselors see more than one person at a time. Couples may see a counselor together. They may deal with issues in their

Talk therapy is not limited to one-on-one sessions between a therapist and patient. It also can involve one therapist meeting with a group of people who are dealing with the same issue and hoping to find support from one another.

relationship, or one partner may give the other support. Sometimes, a group of people with similar problems meets with one therapist. Group members can use one another for support.

Several types of talk therapy are used to treat depression today. Behavioral therapy is one of the most common. It focuses on a person's behaviors and how they are affecting his or her life. By recognizing behaviors that may be contributing to depression, this form of therapy helps people learn to change their behavior.

Cognitive therapy is another very popular type of talk therapy. Negative thoughts can lead to negative feelings and behaviors. This can contribute to depression. It also can make it hard to get better. According to cognitive therapists, depressed people see themselves and their past experiences in negative ways. This keeps them depressed. A cognitive therapist tries to help people change this way of thinking and think more positive thoughts. Cognitive therapy tries to do five things:

1. Help people take notice when they have automatic negative thoughts
2. Use real-life evidence to dispute the negative thoughts
3. Learn different ways to dispute automatic negative thoughts

TALK THERAPY OVER THE PHONE

According to a study released in March 2007, talk therapy given over the phone may work better than therapy done in person. The study was done by the Group Health Cooperative Center in Seattle. Researchers looked at 400 patients who received talk therapy over the telephone. They never met their therapists in person. Most also received antidepressants at the same time. After 18 months, 77% said their depression was either "much better" or "very much better." The researchers pointed out that the people in the study participated in at least six of their scheduled eight sessions of phone-based therapy. People who get therapy in person sometimes don't show up for appointments. One in four people never show up at all. Phone-based therapy, on the other hand, may be easier for people to commit to.

4. Avoid letting negative thoughts repeat in the brain
5. Question the kind of negative thoughts that lead to depression and replace them with positive thoughts that make the person feel good about himself or herself

Another form of talk therapy is called cognitive behavioral therapy, which incorporates some of the techniques of both cognitive and behavioral therapy. This increasingly popular form of therapy encourages patients to take note of their automatic negative thoughts and then change the way they respond to those thoughts in ways that help reduce their depression.

HERBAL REMEDIES

People have been using plants to treat the symptoms of depression since ancient times. Today, there are several herbal remedies that some people use to treat depression. Most herbs and other plants, however, have not been studied scientifically. They do not have to be approved by the FDA before they are sold. So it's not clear whether they work, or even if they are safe. Herbal remedies for depression should be used with caution. Even better, people who want to use these remedies should talk with their doctors about it.

Probably the most popular antidepressant herb is St. John's wort (*Hypericum perforatum*). It has been used for centuries to treat depression, pain, and other problems. Ancient writings contain records of St. John's wort being used as a sedative, as a balm for treating wounds and burns, and as a treatment for **malaria**. Unlike most other herbal remedies, St. John's wort has been subjected to some scientific testing. The studies found it is useful for treating mild to moderate depression.

St. John's wort doesn't cost much. It is easy to get, and it causes fewer side effects than most antidepressant drugs. Some of the side effects that are seen with the use of St. John's wort include:

- Anxiety
- Dizziness
- Dry mouth
- Gastrointestinal problems
- Headache
- Increased sensitivity to sunlight
- Fatigue

St. John's wort may also interact negatively with some drugs. These include warfarin (a drug that thins the blood), birth control pills, other antidepressants, drugs used to treat **HIV**, cancer drugs, drugs that strengthen the heart muscle, and drugs that are used to prevent the body from rejecting transplanted organs.

Another popular remedy for depression is an amino acid called 5-HTP (5-hydroxytryptophan). While it is made naturally in the body, it also can be made from the seeds of a West African plant called *Griffonia simplicifolia*; the plant extract can be bought in a store. Like many antidepressant medications, it is believed to increase levels of serotonin in the brain, easing depression symptoms. It can be used alone, but it is often combined with St. John's wort.

Another alternative remedy for depression is known as SAM-E (S-adenosylmethionine). Discovered in Italy as a treatment for depression in the 1970s, it is also used to treat other conditions, including migraine headaches and fibromyalgia. SAM-E is an amino acid. It helps balance the levels of neurotransmitters in the brain. This regulates mood. Although there is no definitive data on its effects, users have claimed that SAM-E tends to start working within about a week. This is sooner than antidepressant drugs, which may take six weeks to show their effects.

LIGHT THERAPY

Some people have a type of depression known as seasonal affective disorder (SAD). This condition affects approximately 10% of the population. It is more common in places where the days are very short during the winter. People with SAD are fine in the late spring, summer, and early fall. When the days start to get shorter, however, these people become depressed.

One theory says that SAD is related to melatonin. Melatonin is a hormone involved in energy, sleep, and mood. During the short days of winter, some people may produce too much melatonin. This can cause mood changes and depression. Since the mid-1980s, light therapy has been used to combat this form of depression.

Light therapy works by sending visible light into the eyes. From there, a signal goes to the pineal gland, which is the gland that secretes melatonin. This signal tells the pineal gland to make less melatonin. Some people can get outside during winter days and use the sun to treat their SAD symptoms. More often, people use a special lamp or light box. The light given off by the lamp or box needs to be between 5,000 and 10,000 lux (a measure of the intensity of light). This is about the same brightness as a sunny day about 40 minutes after the sun has risen in the morning. People also need to sit close to the light. They keep their eyes open, but do not look directly at the light.

A light box or lamp is used every morning, usually for 30 to 60 minutes. In most cases, the symptoms of SAD begin to get better after a week or so. Some people

Light therapy is used for people with seasonal affective disorder (SAD) who get depressed in the winter when there is less sunlight on Earth. The bright light acts as a replacement for sunlight by helping to reset a person's "body clock."

feel much better after a few weeks. Some medical professionals encourage anyone who thinks they have SAD to use a light box or lamp every day between October and April.

Pregnant women cannot safely take all types of antidepressant drugs or herbal remedies. They can, however, use light therapy without problems.

ACUPUNCTURE

Acupuncture originated in China more than 2,000 years ago. It is used to treat many illnesses, including depression, as well as allergies, pain, and other problems. Acupuncture involves placing very thin needles in the skin at particular points on the body. According to Chinese practitioners, acupuncture works by changing the way energy flows through the body. Scientists have not identified how acupuncture works.

A 1999 study of 34 women with major depression found that after eight weeks of treatment, acupuncture worked as well as antidepressant drugs. More research still needs to be done, but the results of this study were encouraging. About half of the people who ask for treatment for their depression either aren't helped by medication and talk therapy, or stop their treatment before they feel better. Acupuncture may offer an alternative to medication and therapy, especially for pregnant women and those who simply prefer not to take drugs.

AROMATHERAPY

Aromatherapy involves using the scent of special plant oils to relieve the symptoms of certain illnesses. Aromatherapy has been used since ancient times. People who practice aromatherapy say that the oils used are like the hormones of the plant. Just as hormones cause biological changes in the plant, they can cause changes in our bodies.

There hasn't been much research on aromatherapy. But researchers have found that smelling certain scents changes our brain waves. For example, smelling lavender increases alpha waves in the head. This makes people more relaxed. Smelling jasmine appears to increase beta waves. This makes people feel more alert. It is possible that aromatherapy eases depression in similar ways, by reducing mental fatigue, helping patients to sleep better, and elevating mood. Aromatherapy is generally considered most effective when it is not the only type of treatment being used. This is especially true for people with serious cases of depression.

Different essential oils are used to treat various types of depression. For instance, if the depression is the result

The scent of lavender is one of several aromas used in aromatherapy. Research has found that humans find the scent calming, even to the point of making people who smelled it feel drowsy.

of some kind of loss, such as the death of a loved one or a divorce, aromatherapy practitioners normally use oils like marjoram, lavender, rose, hyssop, neroli, and frankincense. For a more general depression, commonly used oils include myrrh, sandalwood, spruce, orange, basil, bergamot, geranium, grapefruit, lemon, and jasmine. Finally, for a depression that has strong symptoms of anger, the aromatherapy oils of choice are usually chamomile, rose, rosemary, and ylang ylang.

ART THERAPY

Art therapy uses art and music to help depressed people express their thoughts and feelings and learn to deal with them. There are as many forms of art therapy as there are forms of art, including painting, dance, poetry,

NUTRITION-BASED THERAPY

Many nutritionists believe that eating the right combinations of foods, exercising, and making certain lifestyle changes can affect serotonin levels in the brain. These practices could ease the symptoms of depression in some people.

Among the diet and lifestyle changes that some experts recommend are:

- Limiting the amount of carbohydrates
- Eating a balanced diet and taking nutritional supplements (such as St. John's wort or SAM-E) as needed to boost serotonin production
- Reducing the use of stimulants (such as caffeine, prescribed drugs with a stimulating effect, and illicit stimulants, such as cocaine)
- Trying to reduce stress
- Exercising regularly, which releases endorphins and helps elevate mood naturally
- Getting enough sunlight exposure (or using a light box or sun lamp to simulate it)

Nutritionists admit that doing all of these things can be more complicated than simply taking a drug. They point out, however, that people who do this have fewer side effects, and that people experience an improvement in their overall health, not just their depression symptoms. This can make a nutrition-based depression treatment more appealing to some people.

and drama. Art therapy appears to be especially good at easing depression among young people. One study showed that having depressed teens create collages, paintings, and other pieces of art helped them to express their feelings in a way that did not make them feel threatened. (Many young people claim to feel threatened or worried about using talk therapy because of the possibility of their parents finding out what they said to therapists.) Using art helped put some distance between the teens and their depression. They could then identify their problems and work with counselors to fix them.

Music therapy is another form of art therapy that is often successful. The American Music Therapy Association (AMTA) says that music therapy is an excellent form of treatment for people who need help communicating about their depression. According to the AMTA, music therapy has many goals, which include:

- Exploring personal feelings, such as self-esteem
- Making changes in mood and emotions to be more positive
- Gaining a sense of control in one's life
- Making a person more aware of the environment and himself or herself
- Improving both verbal and nonverbal expression
- Learning better coping skills and ways to relax
- Supporting healthy thoughts and feelings
- Having social interactions with other people
- Learning better problem-solving skills
- Becoming more independent
- Learning better decision-making skills
- Increasing attention span and the ability to concentrate

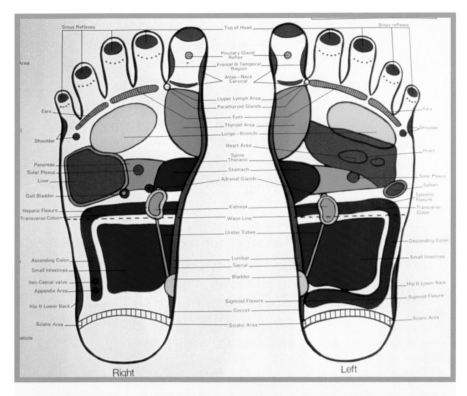

Reflexology is based on the idea that structures of the body have specific reflex zones mapped out over the toes, soles, and sides of feet, and that adding pressure to these zones can help the body feel better. The different colors in the image above represent the different regions, or "reflex zones," found on human feet. Some in the medical community have rejected reflexology, saying it has little or no proven effectiveness.

- Learning to resolve conflicts with family and friends

The type of music depends on the type of problem. To treat depression, most musical therapists have patients listen to slow, relaxing music for at least 20 minutes a day. This seems to slow down the heart rate and help people relax. It also helps them recognize and deal with the causes of their depression symptoms.

OTHER THERAPIES

Researchers continue to study the causes of depression and how they can be treated. As they do this, more alternative therapies are introduced. Some of the most commonly used forms include hypnosis. In hypnosis, a trained professional helps a hypnotized person replace negative thoughts with positive ones.

Reflexology is another treatment that is sometimes used for depression. In this technique, the practitioner applies pressure to specific points on a person's feet. This is supposed to stimulate nerves that are connected to different parts of the body, helping to make the patient feel better.

Some health-care professionals suggest that meditation can be useful in easing depression. Meditation involves entering into a deeply relaxed state by clearing the mind or focusing on a single thought, word, or phrase.

Other people say that exercise is the best remedy for depression. Exercise can affect the levels of certain neurotransmitters, including serotonin and norepinephrine, which may act in a way that is similar to antidepressant drugs to ease depression.

As more research is done on depression and its causes, it is certain that new—and perhaps better—antidepressant remedies will be introduced.

9

The Future of Depression and Antidepressants

Antidepressants can work only if the depressed person takes them. Many people never get that far. They don't know the symptoms of depression, or think they're just feeling a little down. Even when people do visit the doctor for help with the symptoms of depression, their condition is often misdiagnosed. Primary care physicians often try to treat physical symptoms—such as sleep problems and weight changes—without realizing that depression is causing them.

How can you tell if you or someone you know is suffering from depression? The American Psychiatric Association has a very specific list of symptoms to look for:

- You have had an episode of depression that lasted at least two weeks, and you experienced at least five of the following:
  - » Feeling sad, blue, or tearful
  - » Losing interest in things you once enjoyed
  - » Changes in appetite
  - » Trouble sleeping or sleeping too much
  - » Feeling agitated, restless, or sluggish, to an extent that other people have noticed the change
  - » Feeling tired and lacking energy
  - » Feeling worthless or guilty about things you have done or not done
  - » Having trouble concentrating, thinking clearly, or making decisions
  - » Feeling as if you would be better off dead or having thoughts about committing suicide
- The symptoms have been severe enough to affect your daily routine, your work, or your relationships.
- The depression does not have a specific cause, such as physical illness, alcohol or drugs, or a side effect of a medication you are taking.
- The depression is not just a normal reaction to an event such as the death of a loved one.

If you or someone you know has been experiencing these symptoms, you should seek help from your doctor. He or she can determine whether depression is the problem, or if you have a physical disorder that looks like depression. These disorders include a nutrient deficiency or **hypothyroidism**.

GETTING HELP

There are many people and places to turn to for help with depression. All of the following can either treat depression directly or help you find a treatment service:

- Your family doctor
- A psychologist, psychiatrist, counselor, or social worker
- Your insurance provider
- Community health centers
- Hospitals
- Clinics
- Employee assistance programs

DO AFRICAN AMERICANS AVOID GETTING TREATMENT FOR DEPRESSION?

African Americans are less likely than other people to get medical treatment for depression. This finding was discussed at a 2004 meeting of the Black Psychiatrists of America. Annelle Primm, M.D., gave a presentation on the topic.

She said that in general, it's more difficult for African Americans to get high-quality health care, compared with white people. Many black people also do not trust health-care professionals. Some of this distrust may be due to the Tuskegee Project. This was a 40-year research program run by the U.S. government. Researchers studied syphilis—a sexually transmitted disease—by not treating a large group of black men in the South who had the disease. The Tuskegee Project ended in 1972.

- The Web sites of local or national mental health organizations

Besides finding a health-care professional to help with a diagnosis and treatment plan, there are ways you can help yourself or a friend who is depressed.

Helping Yourself When You Are Depressed

People with depression often have negative thoughts. These thoughts usually aren't true. Even if you feel hopeless and like you want to give up, remember that your negative thoughts and feelings probably don't reflect reality.

Another factor that keeps blacks from getting treatment is religion. Many African Americans subscribe to religions that believe that prayer alone—without medical care—can heal people who are suffering from disease or mental health problems.

Finally, Primm said that some African Americans simply believe that suffering is a part of life. They think they should just put up with their depression, rather than get help for it.

Primm developed a video called *Black and Blue* that aims to educate blacks about depression, its symptoms, and the treatments available. It specifically addresses the issue of religion. In it, an African-American pastor says, "As a spiritual man, I look to God. But you know what God is going to do? He's going to send you to a doctor."

Often, when you are feeling depressed, even everyday chores are too much. You can break down larger jobs into smaller tasks and be proud of yourself when you successfully handle even the smallest jobs. Set realistic goals for yourself and work toward fulfilling them. Be with other people as much as possible. It is easy to feel depressed and lonely when you spend too much time alone. Hanging around with friends or family can make you feel better. Go to the movies, play games, or do something outside together. Don't expect to feel better overnight. Be prepared to improve little by little, day by day. Try to think positive thoughts and replace any negative thoughts you may have with positive ones. Don't be afraid to ask your friends and family for help when you need it.

Helping Someone Else Who Is Depressed

Finding professional help and getting an appropriate diagnosis and treatment plan is the most important thing you can do for someone who is depressed. However, that's not all you can do. You can go along with your friend to the doctor, if he or she doesn't want to go alone. You can help make sure your friend remembers to take his or her medicine. You can listen and offer support when your friend wants to talk. You can try to get your friend to go out to the movies, to ball games, or on walks. You can encourage your friend to try a new hobby. In particular, you should try not to judge your friend. Don't assume your friend is just being lazy or is faking depression. Always remember that depression is a very real illness—one that can be life threatening.

FINDING THE RIGHT ANTIDEPRESSANT FOR YOU

There are literally dozens of antidepressants on the market today. Although that might sound like a good thing when you are depressed, finding the right antidepressant to treat a particular person's depression can be very tricky. It can take a lot of time and effort to find the right drug or combination of drugs.

One of the first steps in choosing an antidepressant is for your doctor to look at your general health, including your age, gender, diet, and weight. These can all be factors in picking an antidepressant, mainly because all antidepressants cause different kinds of side effects. It is a good idea to choose a drug with side effects that won't be so difficult to deal with, given your situation and physical condition. People also respond to the various antidepressant drugs in different ways. For example, older adults usually do well on newer classes of antidepressants, such as SSRIs. They don't handle the side effects associated with older antidepressants, such as tricyclics, very well. For this reason, a doctor would be more likely to prescribe an SSRI or SNRI for an older person than a tricyclic or MAOI.

The way an antidepressant is taken can also be a factor in deciding which one is right for you. Although most antidepressant medications are now taken by mouth, a few are still injectable. People who dislike needles would be unlikely to choose those drugs. Most pill-form antidepressants also come in different formulations. Some need to be taken several times a day, whereas others can be taken just once a day or even once a week.

Cost also is important. Many antidepressants are now available in less expensive generic forms. Those available only by brand name can be very expensive.

Once you decide to try a particular antidepressant, you should take the drug consistently for four to eight weeks. This is long enough to find out whether it will work for you. If you haven't noticed improvement after four to eight weeks, consider trying a different drug. And if you do decide to switch drugs, your doctor will talk with you about weaning off the first drug gradually. This helps prevent unpleasant or even dangerous withdrawal symptoms.

In some cases, people simply do not respond to antidepressant drugs at all. Many other forms of treatment—from talk therapy to aromatherapy to shock therapy—can help ease the symptoms of depression instead of drugs.

RECOVERING FROM DEPRESSION

Recovery from depression involves more than just easing symptoms. People with depression want to find a way to ensure that depression doesn't get in the way of their lives. They want to live meaningful lives and reach their full potential. There are five steps to this process.

1. Handling the Impact of the Illness

When someone is depressed, it can affect all aspects of his or her life, including work and relationships with family and friends. In the first stage of recovery, the person learns to recognize how the illness affects his or her life. He or she begins to take steps to reduce that impact. During this stage of recovery, the friends and family of the depressed person can help by offering support, keeping track of the person's symptoms, and being as patient as possible.

2. Feeling as if Life Is Limited

In this stage, the depressed person feels as though his or her life will never be the same. The person may not believe he or she can end the depression and become happy again. The person may feel hopeless. He or she may have distorted thoughts or feelings about the world and his or her life. With proper treatment, the person can learn to change these thoughts. Friends and family can help by being accepting of the person, regardless of how distorted his or her thoughts seem to be. They also can tell the person that he or she can get well.

3. Learning to Believe That Change Is Possible

As a depressed person goes through treatment, he or she begins to think more positively. Hope becomes part of the recovery process. People once again can focus on setting goals and finding little ways to make life better each day. You can help someone get through this stage by helping them develop a healthier lifestyle that includes plenty of exercise, good nutrition, and emotional support. You also can remind them that we all have the power to change our lives. You can help them identify the things they want to change.

4. Committing to Change

In this stage, people begin to see depression as something that can be challenged. They realize that they don't have to define themselves by their depression. As a friend or family member, you can help people in this stage by encouraging them to do things they enjoy, by pointing out their skills and talents, and by supporting them in their efforts to overcome their depression.

5. Taking Action for Change

In this final stage, depressed people learn to move past the power of their illness. They refuse to let it disable their lives. They start meeting the goals they set in previous stages. Many people who successfully overcome depression use this stage to devote themselves to volunteer work, often working with other people who are depressed.

At some point in the future, the depression may come back. As a friend, there are many ways for you to help. You can remind the person that he or she is not alone, that you are there to listen and offer support. You can help the person notice when his or her thinking becomes distorted and take steps to correct it. You also can encourage the person to try to enjoy life by not taking things too seriously.

THE FUTURE OF ANTIDEPRESSANTS

As we have seen, there are many different drugs and alternative therapies available for the treatment of depression. However, most scientists agree that even with all the choices doctors have, the treatment most depressed patients receive is rarely as good as it could be. Sometimes this is because of side effects. Sometimes it's because some medications seem to become less effective over time. This is why researchers are still trying to find new drugs and other treatments for depression.

Many areas of research seem promising. Some scientists are trying to modify antidepressants that are already on the market to make them work better. They might change the way they are taken, or combine more than one drug into a single pill. Many other researchers are looking for ways to prevent the risk of increased suicide that occurs when certain antidepressants are prescribed to young adults.

Other studies are looking into how antidepressant medications work over long periods of time. Many people take antidepressants all the time. There is some concern that the drugs may not work as well after a while. Researchers also wonder if there may be harmful effects that only show up after a longer time period. Some researchers also are looking at what happens to people after they *stop* taking antidepressants. They want to see if depression comes back, and how to prevent this.

Over the last decade, many non-drug treatments have been developed for depression. Among these are

DOCTORS AND DRUG COMPANIES: TOO CLOSE FOR COMFORT?

A May 2007 article in *The New York Times* said that drug companies have been giving money to doctors, particularly psychiatrists. This money has encouraged doctors to prescribe new antidepressants instead of older ones. Some of the new drugs are very expensive. Many people may be taking expensive drugs when they could just as well take ones that cost less and work just as well.

In Minnesota, drug companies must report the amount of money they pay doctors. Between 2000 and 2005, drug companies' payments to doctors in Minnesota increased more than sixfold, to $1.6 million. Doctors who were paid were more likely to prescribe drugs made by the paying drug company. Minnesota doctors who were paid $5,000 or more by companies that manufactured atypical psychotic drugs (a group of drugs used to treat symptoms of **psychosis**) wrote three times as many prescriptions for these drugs as doctors who received less than $5,000 or no money at all.

The *New York Times* article suggested that drug companies are paying doctors to try to control the drugs that patients receive, especially in the mental health industry. Doctors who were interviewed for the story admitted that having a relationship with a drug company could possibly lead them to prescribe a certain drug more often than others. Some observers worry that this might lead doctors to prescribe drugs to people, especially children, for whom they might be dangerous. Doctors might even prescribe drugs to people who don't need them.

vagus nerve stimulation (VNS) and transcranial magnetic stimulation (TMS). VNS was first introduced as a
treatment for epilepsy. It uses an electrical generator to
stimulate the vagus nerve in the head. VNS helps treat
some cases of depression that aren't helped by medications. TMS uses electromagnets placed on a person's
scalp. These create short magnetic pulses, which appear
to help ease depression in some people.

These treatments and others focus on the fact that
every person is different, both in personality and biol-
ogy. As scientists became better able to identify each
person's genetic and biological makeup, drug researchers
hope they will be able to develop better treatment plans
that target each individual's unique form of depression.

GLOSSARY

Acute   Starting suddenly and lasting a short time

Akathisia   A feeling of restlessness and an urge to move

Anesthetic   A drug that makes a person sleepy or fall asleep. Anesthetics are often used when a person needs surgery.

Anorexia nervosa   An eating disorder. People with anorexia nervosa do not eat much. This condition can cause many health problems, and can even be fatal.

Antidepressant   A drug used to ease the symptoms of depression

Antihistamines   Drugs that treat allergy symptoms, such as sneezing and runny nose

Atypical depression   A form of depression. People with atypical depression are hungry more than usual. They also sleep more than is normal and are overly sensitive to rejection.

Benzene   A colorless, flammable, poisonous chemical

Bipolar disorder   A mood disorder. People with bipolar disorder have mood swings. They go from extreme highs, or manias, to being depressed.

Bronchitis   When the breathing tubes in the lungs become swollen

Bulimia   An eating disorder. People with bulimia eat large amounts of food at once. To try to get rid of the food, they then make themselves throw up. Some bulimics use laxatives or exercise a lot instead of vomiting.

Despondent   Extremely sad or discouraged

Diabetes   A disorder in which the body can't move sugar out of the blood and into cells.

Dysthymia   A mood disorder. People with dysthymia have a mild form of depression for years at a time.

Enzyme   A protein that helps start a chemical reaction in the body

Exorcism   A ritual that is supposed to drive out demons from a person or place

Fibromyalgia A disorder in which the muscles and connective tissues (tendons and ligaments) are stiff, tender, and painful

Gastrointestinal Having to do with the stomach or intestines

Half life The amount of time it takes for half of a substance to be broken down or removed from the body

HIV Human immunodeficiency virus; the virus that causes AIDS

Hormone A chemical substance that causes some cells to behave in certain ways

Hypochondriacs People who believe they have diseases that they really don't have

Hypothyroidism An underactive thyroid gland. When the thyroid gland doesn't produce enough thyroid hormone, a person feels sluggish and cold a lot of the time. The body also processes food more slowly.

Insomnia Trouble falling or staying asleep

Jaundice A condition in which the skin and the whites of the eyes turn yellow. Jaundice usually is a symptom of liver disease.

Lithium A chemical element that is often used to stabilize mood

Malaria A disease spread by mosquitoes. Malaria causes chills and fever.

Manic Elated, hyperactive, often impulsive

Melancholia An old-fashioned term for *depression*

Migraines Severe headaches

Mucous membranes The linings of body cavities and passages, such as the nose, throat, lungs, and intestines

Mysticism The belief that people can experience direct communion with God

Neurons Nerve cells in the brain

Neurotransmitters   Chemicals that act as messengers, sending signals from one brain cell to another

Postpartum depression (PPD)   A depressed state that occurs within a year after a woman gives birth to a child

Prefrontal cortex   Part of the front of the brain. The prefrontal cortex is involved that in complex thinking, emotions, and behavior.

Psychoanalysis   A system of talk therapy that theorizes that a person's problems can be traced to his or her past experiences

Psychosis   A condition in which a person loses contact with reality and may suffer hallucinations or delusions

Psychotropic   Acting on the mind

Reuptake   When a neurotransmitter is taken back inside a neuron after a chemical message has been sent

Seasonal affective disorder (SAD)   A depressed state that occurs in the fall and winter, when the days are shorter

Schizophrenia   A mental disorder in which people see and hear things that are not actually there and believe things that are not true.

Shingles   A viral disease that causes painful skin outbreaks

Specters   Ghosts

Stasis   Staying the same

Stigma   A mark of shame

Stimulant   Something that causes the body's processes to speed up

Synapses   The spaces between neurons

Tuberculosis   A contagious lung disease

Unipolar   A mood disorder in which a person only experiences depression, not mania

BIBLIOGRAPHY

BOOKS

Ainsworth, Patricia. *Understanding Depression*. Jackson, MS: University Press of Mississippi, 2000.

Depression and Bipolar Support Alliance. *Introduction to Depression and Bipolar Disorder*. Chicago: Depression and Bipolar Support Alliance, 2003.

Kramer, Peter D. *Listening to Prozac*. New York: Penguin Books, 1997.

Miletich. John J. *Depression: A Multimedia Sourcebook*. Westport, CT: Greenwood Press, 1995.

Shorter, Edward. *A History of Psychiatry: From the Era of the Asylum to the Age of Prozac*. New York: John Wiley & Sons, 1997.

Solomon, Andrew. *The Noonday Demon*. New York: Scribner, 2001.

Styron, William. *Darkness Visible: A Memoir of Madness*. New York: Vintage Books, 1992.

Taylor, Michael Alan, and Max Fink. *Melancholia: The Diagnosis, Pathophysiology and Treatment of Depressive Illness*. New York: Cambridge University Press, 2006.

Torrey, E. Fuller, and Michael B. Knable. *Surviving Manic Depression*. New York: Basic Books, 2002.

Wider, Paul. *Overcoming Depression and Manic Depression*. Rutherford, NJ: Wellness Communications, 2001.

ARTICLES

Baldwin, David, and Chris Thompson. "The Future of Antidepressant Pharmacotherapy." *World Psychiatry*. February 2003. pp. 3–8.

Bosker, F. J. et al. "Future Antidepressants: What Is in the Pipeline and What Is Missing?" *CNS Drugs*. 2004. pp. 705–732.

Currie, Janet. "The Marketization of Depression: The Prescribing of SSRI Antidepressants to Women." *Women and Health Protection*. May 2005.

Garnett, Leah R. "Prozac Revisited." *Boston Globe*. May 7, 2000.

Greenhouse, Joel B., and Kelly J. Kelleher. "Thinking Outside the (Black) Box: Antidepressants, Suicidality, and Research Synthesis." *Pediatrics*. July 2005. pp. 231–233.

Harris, Gardiner, Benedict Carey, and Janet Roberts. "Psychiatrists, Children and Drug Industry's Role." *The New York Times*. May 10, 2007.

Lieberman, Joseph A. "History of the Use of Antidepressants in Primary Care." *Journal of Clinical Psychiatry*. 2003 (5) (suppl 7). pp. 6–10.

Marsa, Linda. "Non-Drug Alternatives in Depression Treatment." *Los Angeles Times*. July 30, 2002.

Moran, Mark. "Culture, History Can Keep Blacks From Getting Depression Treatment." *Psychiatric News*. June 4, 2004. p. 12.

Pollack, M. H. "Abstract on Symptoms and Treatment of Social Anxiety Disorder." *Journal of Clinical Psychiatry*. 2001 (62)(suppl 12): pp. 24–29.

Reinberg, Steven. "Antidepressants Linked to Fracture Risk." *The Washington Post*. January 22, 2007.

Riley, Shirley. "Art Therapy with Adolescents." *Western Journal of Medicine*. July 2001. pp. 54–57.

Rosack, Jim. "Transdermal Patch Could Herald Renewed Popularity for MAOIs." *Psychiatric News*. December 6, 2002. p. 43.

Schechter, Lee E. et al. "Innovative Approaches for the Development of Antidepressant Drugs." *NeuroRx*. October 2005. pp. 590–611.

WEB SITES

Acupuncture Helps Depression. Health Education Alliance for Life and Longevity. http://www.heall.com/body/altmed/treatment/disease/psychological/depression/acupuncturehelpsdepression.html.

All About Depression. PsychCentral. September 7, 2006. http://psychcentral.com/library/depression_general.htm.

Alternative and Complementary Therapies for Depression. Holistic Online. http://www.holistitconline.com/Remedies/Depression/dep_home.htm.

American Psychiatric Associaion. Accessed January 2, 2008. http://www.psych.org/.

Antidepressants. http://www.indepression.com/antidepressants.html.

Antidepressants: Another Weapon Against Chronic Pain. CNN.com. http://www.cnn.com/HEALTH/library/PN/00044.html.

Antidepressants, tricyclic. Health A to Z. http://www.healthatoz.com/healthatoz/Atoz/common/standard/transform.jsp?requestURI=/healthatoz/Atoz/ency/antidepressants_tricyclic.jsp.

Antidepressants: The Tricyclics. St. Louis Psychologist and Counseling Information and Referral. http://www.psychtreatment.com/antidepressants_tricyclics.htm.

Aromatherapy. Holistic Online. http://www.holisticonline.com/Aromatherapy/aroma_what_is.htm.

Barclay, Laurie. "Selective Serotonin Reuptake Inhibitors May Reduce Risk for Colon Cancer." http://www.medscape.com/viewarticle/528728.

Boyles, Salynn. Drugs, 'Shock Therapy' Beat Depression: Study Shows ECT and Antidepressants Are Effective Therapies. FoxNews.com. http://www.webmd.com/depression/news/20060112/drugs-shock-therapy-beat-depression.

———. Study Links Depression and Pain. Depression Health Center. 2004. http://www.webmd.com/depression/news/20040826/study-links-depression-pain.

Buproban. MedTV. http://mental-health.emedtv.com/buproban/buproban.html.

Center for the Advancement of Children's Mental Health. Serotonin Reuptake Inhibitors. http://www.kidsmentalhealth.org/SSRI.html.

Cognitive Therapy. Holistic Online. http://www.holisticonline.com/remedies/Depression/dep_treatment_cognitive_treatment.htm.

Depression and Aromatherapy. Depression-Guide.com. http://www.depression-guide.com/aromatherapy-depression.htm.

Depression and Bipolar Support Alliance. Depression: The Unwanted Cotraveler. March 2001. http://www.dbsalliance.org/site/PageServer?pagename=edia_speeches_cotraveler.

———. Facts About Depression. January 2, 2007. http://www.dbsalliance.org/site/PageServer?pagename=FAQ#WhatDepression.

———. Recovery Steps. May 10, 2006. http://www.dbsalliance.org/site/PageServer?pagename=recoverysteps.htm.

———. Types of Depression. March 12, 2007. http://www.dbsalliance.org/site/PageServer?pagename=about_MDOverview.

Depression and the Effects on Business. iFred: Shining the Light on Depression. http://www.ifred.org/ifacts.html.

Depression Health Center. Alternative Therapies for Depression. http://www.webmd.com/depression/alternative-therapies-depression.

Diagnosing Depression. Holistic Online.com. http://www.holisticonline.com/Remedies/Depression/dep_diagnosis_1.htm.

Ekeruo, Wesley. Depression—Its Nature, Historical Perception, Signs and Symptoms, and Preventative Measures.

May 6, 1999. http://sulcus.berkeley.edu/mcb/165_001/papers/maunscripts/_52.html.

Eternal Sunshine. The Observer. http://observer.guardian.co.uk/print/0,,329819920–110648,00.html.

Fibromyalgia Health Center. Serotonin and Norepineph-rine Reuptake Inhibitors for Fibromyalgia. Fox News.com. http://www.webmd.com/fibromyalgia/guide/fibromyalgia-medications.

Fluoxetine. MedlinePlus. http://www.nlm.nih.gov/medlineplus/druginfo/medmaster/a689006.html.

Food and Drug Administration. Questions and Answers on Antidepressant Use in Children, Adolescents, and Adults. http://www.fda.gov/cder/drug/antidepressant/QA20070502.htm.

———. Suicidality in Children and Adolescents Being Treated With Antidepressant Medications. October 14, 2004. http://www.fda.gov/cder/drug/antidepressants/SSRIPHA200410.htm.

Hasselbring, Bobbie. Tetracyclic Antidepressants. Depression Center. http://health.discovery.com/articles-123/c09/LC_37/p06.shtml.

Hastings, C. Devin. The Role of Hypnosis in the Cause and Cure of Depression. Depression and Hypnosis. http://www.depression-hypnosis.com/treatment.htm.

Herbal Treatments for Depression. Amoryn Means Happiness. http://www.amoryn.com/zzherbaltreatmentfordepression.html.

Hirsch, Michael, and Robert J. Birnbaum. Antidepressant Medication in Adults: Tricyclics and Tetracyclics. Up to Date Patient Information. http://patients.uptodate.com/topic.asp?file=psychiat/14445.

History of Mental Illness and Treatments. Psychological Therapies. http://web.umr.edu/~pfyc212b/Therapy.htm.

Light Therapy for Seasonal Affective Disorders. Holistic Online. http://www.holisticonline.com/Light_Therapy/light_SAD.htm.

MAOI Inhibitor. Depression-Guide.com. http://www.depression-guide.com/maoi-inhibitors.htm.

Mayo Clinic. Antidepressants: Selecting One That's Right for You. Accessed December 8, 2006. http://www.mayoclinic.com/health/antidepressants/HQ01069.

———. Combined Reuptake Inhibitors and Receptor Blockers. Accessed December 8, 2006. http://www.mayoclinic.com/print/mental-health/MH00070.

———. Fibromyalgia. Accessed December 8, 2006. http://www.mayoclinic.com/health/fibromyalgia/DS00079.

———. Monoamine Oxidase Inhibitors. Accessed December 8, 2006. http://www.mayoclinic.com/print/maois/MH00072.

———. Norepinephrine and Dopamine Reuptake Inhibitors. Accessed December 8, 2006. http://www.mayoclinic.com/health/antidepressants/MH00068.

———. Psychotherapy: An Overview of the Types of Therapy. Accessed December 8, 2006. http://www.mayoclinic.com/health/psychotherapy/MH00009.

———. Selective Serotonin Reuptake Inhibitors. Accessed December 8, 2006. http://www.mayoclinic.com/health/ssris/MH00066.

———. Serotonin and Norepinephrine Reuptake Inhibitors. Accessed December 8, 2006. http://www.mayoclinic.com/health/antidepressants/MH00067.

———. Tetracyclic Antidepressants. Accessed December 8, 2006. http://www.mayoclinic.com/health/mental-health/MH00069.

———. Tricyclic Antidepressants. Accessed December 8, 2006. http://www.mayoclinic.com/health/antidepressants/MH00071.

Mirtzapine. How Stuff Works. Accessed January 2, 2008. http://www.howstuffworks.com/define-mirtzapine.htm.

Monoamine Oxidase Inhibitors. Healthy Place.com. Accessed January 2, 2008. http://www.healthyplace.com/Communities/Depression/treatment/antidepressants/maoi.asp.

Montgomery, Stuart A. Selective Serotonin Reuptake Inhibitors in the Acute Treatment of Depression. Accessed January 2, 2008. http://www.acnp.org/g4/GN401000102/CH100.html.

My Personal Story of Recovery. Depression-Recovery-Life. Accessed July 2, 2007. http://www.depression-recovery-life.com/personal-story.html.

National Alliance on Mental Illness. About Mental Illness. 1996–2007. Accessed January 2, 2008. http://www.nami.org/Content/NavigationMenu/Inform_Yourself/About_Mental_Illness/About_Mental_Illness.htm.

————. People with Mental Illness Enrich Our Lives. 1996–2007. Accessed January 2, 2008. http://www.nami.org/Template.cfm?Section=Helpline1&template=/Content Management/ContentDisplay.cfm&ContentID=4858.

————. Understanding Major Depression and Recovery. Arlington, VA: National Alliance on Mental Illness, National Center for Complementary and Alternative Medicine. St. John's Wort. Herbs at a Glance. Accessed January 2, 2008. http://nccam.nih.gov/health/stjohnswort/.

Neurobiology of Depression. Accessed January 2, 2008. http://www.sci.sdsu.edu/classes/psychology/psy760/handouts/depression.htm.

News in Science. Analysis: Gaps Revealed in Antidepressant Research. ABC.com. May 30, 2003. Accessed January 2, 2008. http://www.abc.net.au/science/news/health/HealthRepublish_867510.htm.

NIH News. New NIMH Research Strives to Understand How Antidepressants May Be Associated With Suicidal Thoughts and Actions. November 13, 2006. Accessed January 2, 2008. http://www.nih.gov/news/pr/nov2006/nimh-13.htm.

Palmer, Ann. 20th Century History of the Treatment of Mental Illness: A Review. Accessed January 2, 2008. http://www.mentalhealthworld.org/29ap.html.

Payk, T. R. Historical Treatment of Depression. The Delano Report. Accessed January 2, 2008. http://www.delano.com/ReferenceArticles/Depression-Historical.html.

Phone-based Therapy Eases Depression Long Term. Science Daily. March 27, 2007. Accessed January 2, 2008. http://www.sciencedaily.com/releases/2007/03/070322105358.htm.

Pick, Marcelle. Antidepressants and Alternative Treatments for Depression. Women to Women. Accessed January 2, 2008. http://www.womentowomen.com/depressionanxietymood/antidepressants.asp.

Price, Prentiss. Getting Help for Depression. All About Depression. September 9, 2004. Accessed January 2, 2008. http://www.allaboutdepression.com/tre_01.html.

Prozac: Indications & Dosage. RXList: The Internet Drug Index. Accessed January 2, 2008. http://www.rxlist.com/cgi/generic/fluoxetine_ids.htm.

Prozac Side Effects. The Linden Method. Accessed January 2, 2008. http://www.panic-anxiety.com/prozac_side_effect/prozac_side_effect.htm.

Read, Kimberly, and Marcia Purse. Monoamine Oxidase Inhibitors. About.com: Bipolar Disorder. Accessed January 2, 2008. http://bipolar.about.com/od/maois/a/maois_profile.htm.

———. Self-medication: When the Cure Is the Disease. About.com: Bipolar Disorder. Accessed January 2, 2008. http://bipolar.about.com/cs/dualdiag/a/0008_dual_diag.htm?p=1.

Selective Serotonin Reuptake Inhibitors. HealthyPlace.com. Accessed January 2, 2008. http://www.healthyplace.com/Communities/Depression/treatment/antidepressants/index.asp.

Serotonin and Noradrenaline Reuptake Inhibitors. Patient Plus. Accessed January 2, 2008. http://www.patient.co.uk/showdoc/40024938/.

Sound and Music Therapy. Holistic Online. Accessed January 2, 2008. http://www.holisticonline.com/Remedies/Depression/dep_sound_therapy.htm.

Svoboda, Elizabeth. Shock Therapy, Version 2.0. Wired. February 1, 2006. Accessed January 2, 2008. http://www.wired.com/print/science/discoveries/news/2006/02/70085.

Tong, Theodore G. What Foods You Should Avoid on MAOIs. Accessed January 2, 2008. http://deoxy.org/maoidiet.htm.

Treating Depression Naturally—Herbal Treatment. Depression-Guide.com. Accessed January 2, 2008. http://www.depression-guide.com/herbal-remedy-for-depression.htm.

Treating Depression With Acupuncture. Special Focus. Accessed January 2, 2008. http://www.acupuncture-online.com/depression.html.

Treatment and Therapy—Pain Medication. Jack Miller Center for Peripheral Neuropathy. Accessed January 2, 2008. http://millercenter.uchicago.edu/learnaboutpn/treatment/.

Tricyclic Antidepressants. Accessed January 2, 2008. http://www.intelihealth.com/IH/ihtIH/WSIHW000/8596/35229/363019.html?d=dmtContent.

Tricyclic Antidepressants. Accessed January 2, 2008. http://www.patient.co.uk/showdoc/23068678/.

Tricyclic Antidepressants—A Risk Factor for Epilepsy? Neurology Reviews.com. April 2000. Accessed January 2, 2008. http://www.neurologyreviews.com/apr00/nr_apr00_antidepressants.html.

Tricyclic Related Antidepressants. Overcome Depression. Accessed January 2, 2008. http://www.overcomedepression.co.uk/TricyclicRelatedAntidepressants.html.

Trujillo, Keith A., and Andrea B. Chinn. Antidepressants. Drugs and the Brain. Accessed January 2, 2008. http://www.csusm.edu/DandB/AD.html.

U.S. Department of Health & Human Services. Depression During and After Pregnancy. Womenshealth.gov. April 2005. Accessed January 2, 2008. http://www.womenshealth.gov/faq/postpartum.htm.

Watkins, Carol E. Seasonal Affective Disorder and Light Therapy. Seasonal Affective Disorder: Winter Depression. December 11, 2004. Accessed January 2, 2008. http://www.ncpamd.com/seasonal.htm.

Zyban. QuitSmoking.com. Accessed January 2, 2008. http://www.quitsmoking.com/zyban/index.htm.

FURTHER READING

BOOKS

Docalavich, Heather. *The Future of Antidepressants*. Broomall, PA: Mason Crest Publishers, 2006.

Dudley, William, ed. *The History of Drugs—Antidepressants*. San Diego: Greenhaven Press, 2004.

Dunbar, Katherine Read. *Antidepressants (At Issue Series)*. San Diego: Greenhaven Press, 2005.

Esherick, Joan. *Prozac: North American Culture and the Wonder Drug*. Broomall, PA: Mason Crest Publishing, 2006.

Kramer, Peter D. *Listening to Prozac*. New York: Penguin Books, 1997.

Levert, Suzanne. *The Facts About Antidepressants*. New York: Benchmark Books, 2006.

Mitchell, E. Siobhan. *Antidepressants (Drugs: The Straight Facts)*. Philadelphia: Chelsea House Publishers, 2004.

Packard, Helen C. *Prozac: The Controversial Cure*. New York: Rosen Publishing Group, 1999.

Wurtzel, Elizabeth. *Prozac Nation*. Topeka, KS: Tandem Library, 1999.

WEB SITES

ANTIDEPRESSANTS FACTS

http://www.antidepressantsfacts.com/

This site provides information about Prozac and other antidepressants, including details on how they work, places for people with mental illness to turn for support, and information about side effects.

FLUOXETINE (MARKETED AS PROZAC) INFORMATION

http://www.fda.gov/Cder/Drug/infopage/fluoxetine/default.htm

This site is run by the U.S. Food and Drug Administration. It provides information and warnings that involve Prozac.

THE MAYO CLINIC

http://www.mayoclinic.com/health/SEARCH/Search

This page from the Mayo Clinic provides links to several articles that deal with antidepressants and their proper use and side effects.

DRUG INFORMATION ONLINE

http://www.drugs.com/prozac.html

This site provides information about how Prozac works and what side effects and dangers users may face.

ELI LILLY'S PROZAC.COM

http://www.prozac.com/index.jsp

This is the official drug site for Prozac, sponsored by Eli Lilly, the pharmaceutical company that manufactures Prozac.

PROZAC (FLUOXETINE)

http://www.nami.org/Template.cfm?Section=About_ Medications&Template=/TaggedPage/TaggedPageDisplay.cfm&TPLID=5 1&ContentID=20817

This page is part of the Web site for the National Alliance on Mental Illness (NAMI). It provides information about Prozac and issues associated with its use.

PHOTO CREDITS

INDEX

ABOUT THE AUTHORS

TARA KOELLHOFFER earned a degree in political science and history from Rutgers University. Today, she is a freelance writer and editor with more than 12 years of experience working on nonfiction books, covering topics ranging from social studies and biography to health and science. She has edited hundreds of books and teaching materials, including a history of Italy published by Greenhaven Press and the *Science News for Kids* series published by Chelsea House. She lives in Pennsylvania.

Series introduction author **RONALD J. BROGAN** is the Bureau Chief for the New York City office of D.A.R.E. (Drug Abuse Resistance Education) America, where he trains and coordinates more than 100 New York City police officers in program-related activities. He also serves as a D.A.R.E. regional director for Oregon, Connecticut, Massachusetts, Maine, New Hampshire, New York, Rhode Island, and Vermont. In 1997, Brogan retired from the U.S. Drug Enforcement Administration (DEA), where he served as a special agent for 26 years. He holds bachelor's and master's degrees in criminal justice from the City University of New York.